# Dividend Growth Investing and Portfolio Management

## Use the Power of Dividend Growth to Create a Winning Portfolio

G. R. Tiberius

# SPECIAL FEATURED BOOK

## *(Scan QR Code to access)*

# SPECIAL FEATURED BOOK

*(Scan QR Code to access)*

# SPECIAL FEATURED BOOK

*(Scan QR Code to access)*

TO MY WIFE AND MY SON, THIS BOOK IS FOR YOU.

© **Copyright 2023 - All rights reserved.**

The content contained within this book may not be reproduced, duplicated or transmitted without direct written permission from the author or the publisher.

Under no circumstances will any blame or legal responsibility be held against the publisher, or author, for any damages, reparation, or monetary loss due to the information contained within this book, either directly or indirectly.

Legal Notice:

This book is copyright protected. It is only for personal use. You cannot amend, distribute, sell, use, quote or paraphrase any part, or the content within this book, without the consent of the author or publisher.

Disclaimer Notice:

Please note the information contained within this document is for educational and entertainment purposes only. All effort has been executed to present accurate, up to date, reliable, complete information. No warranties of any kind are declared or implied. Readers acknowledge that the author is not engaged in the rendering of legal, financial, medical or professional advice. The content within this book has been derived from various sources. Please consult a licensed professional before attempting any techniques outlined in this book.

By reading this document, the reader agrees that under no circumstances is the author responsible for any losses, direct or indirect, that are incurred as a result of the use of the information contained within this document, including, but not limited to, errors, omissions, or inaccuracies.

# Table of Contents

**INTRODUCTION** .................................................................................. 1

**CHAPTER 1: BRIEF INTRODUCTION TO DIVIDENDS** ............................. 5

    WHAT ARE DIVIDENDS? ........................................................................ 6
        *Understanding How Dividends Work* ................................................ 6
        *Types of Dividends* ........................................................................... 7
    WHY ARE DIVIDENDS IMPORTANT FOR SHAREHOLDERS? ........................ 8
        *Overall Growth and Profits* .............................................................. 8
        *Equity Valuation* .............................................................................. 9
        *Reduction of Risk* ........................................................................... 10
        *Tax Benefits* ................................................................................... 10
        *Purchasing Power* ......................................................................... 11
    CHOOSING THE BEST DIVIDEND STOCKS ............................................... 11

**CHAPTER 2: DIVIDEND INVESTING: THE BEGINNING** ....................... 15

    UNDERSTANDING DIVIDEND INVESTING ............................................... 15
        *How Does Dividend Investing Work?* ............................................ 16
        *Is Dividend Investing Safe?* ........................................................... 17
    KEY METRICS TO UNDERSTAND DIVIDEND INVESTING ........................... 17
    STRATEGIES FOR DIVIDEND INVESTING ................................................ 20
    DOES DIVIDEND INVESTING HELP YOU WITH YOUR TAXES? ................... 21
    CHALLENGES OF DIVIDEND INVESTING (AND HOW TO OVERCOME THEM) ....... 22

**CHAPTER 3: DIVIDEND MODELS** ..................................................... 25

    DIVIDEND GROWTH MODEL ................................................................ 25
        *Gordon Growth Model* .................................................................. 26
    CALCULATION OF DIVIDEND GROWTH RATE ......................................... 28
    DIVIDEND DISCOUNTING MODEL .......................................................... 31
        *What Is the Dividend Discounting Model?* ................................... 31

**CHAPTER 4: DIVIDEND GROWTH INVESTING** .................................. 33

    WHAT DOES DIVIDEND GROWTH INVESTING MEAN? ............................ 34
        *How to Choose the Right Growth Stocks?* .................................... 34
        *Dividends Are Great Indicators of Returns* ................................... 35
        *Limitations of Dividend Growth Investing* .................................... 35
    DIVIDEND YIELD VS. DIVIDEND GROWTH ............................................. 36
        *What Is Dividend Yield?* ................................................................ 37

  *What Is Dividend Growth?*..................................................................*38*
  *Growth Is an Indication That the Operating Environment Is Healthy*..........*39*

## CHAPTER 5: DIVIDEND GROWTH INVESTING STRATEGIES.............................. 41

 STRATEGIES TO FOLLOW ...................................................................................42
  *Which Strategy Is Useful for You?* ......................................................*44*

## CHAPTER 6: PORTFOLIO MANAGEMENT............................................................ 45

 WHAT IS PORTFOLIO MANAGEMENT? ................................................................46
  *Process of Portfolio Management* ....................................................*47*
  *Active and Passive Portfolio Management*........................................*49*
 RISK APPETITE AND RISK TOLERANCE ................................................................50
  *What Is Risk Appetite?*......................................................................*51*
  *What Is Risk Tolerance?*....................................................................*51*
  *Relationship Between Risk Appetite and Risk Tolerance* ....................*52*
 THE CONCEPT OF BETA......................................................................................52
  *Understanding Beta*..........................................................................*53*
  *Importance of Beta*...........................................................................*54*
  *Beta of Your Portfolio* .......................................................................*55*
  *Why You Should be Careful While Analyzing Beta* ............................*55*

## CHAPTER 7: INVESTMENT TIPS IN CHANGING SITUATIONS............................... 57

 SOME GENERAL INVESTMENT TIPS ....................................................................58
  *How Is Dividend Growth Investing Different?* ..................................*58*
  *The Benefit of Compounding* ...........................................................*59*
 INVESTING STRATEGIES FOR A BEAR MARKET......................................................60
  *Don't Let Fear Take Over You* ..........................................................*61*
  *Dollar Cost Averaging* ......................................................................*61*
  *Play Dead*.........................................................................................*62*
  *Diversify According to Your Affordability* ........................................*62*
  *Search for Values*.............................................................................*62*
  *Search for Defensive Industries* ........................................................*63*
  *Include Some Cash*...........................................................................*63*
  *Find a Financial Consultant* .............................................................*63*

## CONCLUSION ...................................................................................................... 65

## CHAPTER 8: BONUS CHAPTER 1: RETIREMENT .................................................. 69

 FACTORS TO CONSIDER FOR RETIREMENT PLANNING...........................................70
  *Time Horizon*....................................................................................*70*
  *Retirement Spending Needs* .............................................................*70*
  *Assess Your Risk Tolerance* ..............................................................*71*
  *Estate Planning*................................................................................*71*
 STEPS TO RETIREMENT PLANNING .....................................................................71

INVESTMENT PLANS FOR RETIREMENT ........................................................................ 73
   *Defined Contribution Plans* .......................................................................... 74
   *IRAs* ................................................................................................................ 74
   *Traditional Pensions* ..................................................................................... 75
   *401(k) Plans* .................................................................................................. 75
   *Cash Value Insurance Plan* ............................................................................ 76
   *Investment in Long-Term Stocks* .................................................................. 76
   *Dividend Investing* ........................................................................................ 76

**CHAPTER 9: BONUS CHAPTER 2: REITS ........................................................... 77**
   UNDERSTANDING REITs .......................................................................................... 78
      *How do REITs Work?* ..................................................................................... 78
      *Types of REITs* ............................................................................................... 79
      *What Can Qualify as a REIT?* ........................................................................ 80
   PROS AND CONS OF INVESTING IN REITs ................................................................. 81
      *Pros* ................................................................................................................ 81
      *Cons* .............................................................................................................. 82
   REIT FRAUD ........................................................................................................... 83

**GLOSSARY ........................................................................................................ 85**

**REFERENCES ................................................................................................... 101**
   IMAGE REFERENCES ............................................................................................. 106

# Introduction

Investing is a tricky business. Most people venture into this field without proper knowledge or experience about where to put their money and why. There are thousands of stocks trading in the stock markets of all countries and it can often be overwhelming to understand which one is suitable for you. If you run a quick search on the Internet, you will find a list of stocks that might be "good for trading" or "earn good dividends."

For new investors, the time horizon is often confusing because they want to make profits from their stocks but also want capital appreciation. Although these two might sound conflicting, there is a way you can achieve both. Dividend stocks can help you grow your portfolio and make good profits over a long period. There is a general misconception that dividend stocks are only for risk-averse or retired people. This is not true and you can easily turn your dividend stocks into genuinely profitable ones by dividend growth investing.

When you want to make good money and create wealth, you have to turn to stock markets. Instruments like bonds will only help you reach your savings goals but if you are looking for genuine appreciation, stocks are the way to go. Dividend stocks have traditionally been considered safe instruments that will help you to grow your money over time. However, with the help of dividend growth investing, you will be able to turn that safe investment into a highly profitable instrument.

Dividends should not just be considered as the extra income that you receive for holding a stock. Instead, they should be perceived as profit units that will help in capital growth and short-term gains. My investing journey began more than six years ago and ever since then, I have been passionate about teaching the world about the wonders that dividend investing can bring about. I wish to build a retirement nest egg that will help me achieve financial independence. I want my retirement fund to last a lifetime and I want to use passive income as the vehicle to create the life I have always dreamed of. In my previous book, *Dividend Investing for Beginners*, I gave an overview of what dividends are and how you can select a suitable dividend stock. Before you start reading this book, I would suggest you go through the previous one so that you know everything about the basics of dividends.

Dividend growth is a very important concept in the context of investing and capital appreciation. In this book, we will delve deeper into the nuances of dividend growth investing and how you can make a lot of profit even with dividend stocks.

I am passionate about teaching readers how they can utilize the power of dividend growth for enhancing their investment portfolio like never before. One of the biggest problems of investment advice is that it might not stay relevant after a few years. That is why I have curated this book for the long term. All the advice you receive through this book (just like my previous one) will remain valid. The outbreak of the COVID-19 pandemic and the subsequent widespread economic devastation has shown us that the world is extremely vulnerable to sudden changes and we have to make provisions to be prepared for them. The economy has taken a downturn throughout the world which makes it very important for us to have a strategy that will be applicable in all kinds of situations.

If you can truly adopt dividend growth investing, regardless of any crisis or challenges, your portfolio will keep growing over time. I will discuss everything about the rationale behind dividend growth so that you can have a sound theoretical background about dividends before you think about investing in them. We will talk about dividend growth models and portfolio management strategies which will give you a clear insight into how the whole process works.

So let's jump right into the fascinating world of dividend growth investing and help you learn all the tricks of the trade. Happy reading!

Chapter 1:

# Brief Introduction to Dividends

Owning a stock in a company means that you become its part-owner. Just like all owners, you have to undertake certain risks that come with instabilities in the market or performance issues. However, as an owner, you also get to enjoy the fruits of profits and growth. Companies often reward their shareholders with dividends as a means to share the profit that they have earned.

When you are thinking about long-term investments and growth, dividend-paying stocks are the best choice. In my previous book *Dividend Investing for Beginners*, I went into great detail about the concept of dividends and how you can choose the best dividend-paying stocks. Here, we will attempt to scale up our knowledge regarding dividends and have an advanced conversation about how they can become an integral part of your investment portfolio.

In this chapter, we will brush up on the basics of dividends so that you feel prepared to move ahead and use them diligently in your investing journey.

# What Are Dividends?

Dividends are the distribution of a company's earnings to its shareholders either in the form of cash or reinvestment in more stocks of the company (Hayes, 2022). Usually, dividends are paid every quarter (although this is not a fixed rule) and if you own the shares before the date of dividend declaration, you will be eligible for the same.

In any company, the declaration and distribution of dividends are determined by the board of directors and approved by the shareholders who have voting rights. This is done to ensure that the majority of the shareholders agree to the decision of paying out dividends.

## *Understanding How Dividends Work*

Investors are often confused regarding the rationale that a company follows for the determination of dividends. Before you start investing in dividend stocks, it is important to understand the logic behind them. Consider the following example for clarity.

Suppose you hold eight shares of Apple Inc which comes to around $1,000. When Apple Inc earns a profit, the board of directors can decide to share it with the shareholders in the form of dividends. Depending upon company policy, they can decide to distribute such dividends as cash or additional units of shares. For instance, dividends can be paid at a specified rate of the company's share price. In this case, if Apple decides to pay 2% dividend, then you will receive $20 (2% of $1,000). The company can also decide to distribute dividends in a specific ratio like 4:1 when they would pay one share as a dividend for every four shares held by the shareholder. In that case, you would end up receiving two extra shares as dividends (¼ of eight shares).

Every company has to follow a distinct set of rules and regulations for the declaration and distribution of dividends to ensure all the eligible shareholders are receiving their shares.

## *Types of Dividends*

Usually, a company pays the following types of dividends:

- **Cash Dividend:** The most common types of dividends are cash dividends paid to the shareholders in the form of cash that is sent directly to the shareholder's accounts (O'Shea & Lam-Balfour, 2022).

- **Stock Dividend:** Companies often decide to pay dividends in the form of additional stocks to the existing shareholders. These dividends are known as stock dividends.

- **Dividend Reinvestment Programs (DRIPs):** Dividend Reinvestment Programs (DRIPs) are special schemes created by companies where shareholders can reinvest shares that they have received as dividends. Such reinvestment will be done at a discount, which means that the shareholder will be able to procure more shares at a lesser price. DRIPs are not mandatory for the shareholder, and they usually have the choice of accepting the dividends in cash.

- **Special Dividends:** Special dividends are paid out of extraordinary earnings that the company does not need to accumulate anymore (O'Shea & Lam-Balfour, 2022). The company might have earned such income a long time ago and they want to put it to good use by distributing a special dividend on all classes of stocks. Unlike normal dividends, special dividends are not distributed at regular frequencies.

- **Preferred Dividends:** These are dividends that are paid to holders of preferred stocks.

# Why Are Dividends Important for Shareholders?

As an investor who is thinking about including dividend investing in their portfolio, you should have clarity about why dividends matter. Are they simply additional payments that you receive as an incentive for holding shares of a particular company, or is there some other significance attached to it?

Dividends can be valuable additions to your investment portfolio and help you in growing wealth over the years. Here are a few reasons why dividends are important for shareholders and why you should choose stocks that pay dividends.

## *Overall Growth and Profits*

When you are investing in the stock market, you have to understand that there is a certain amount of inherent risk associated with every equity investment. Although the general notion is that all stocks tend to increase in value over time, there is no guarantee of the same. This is an assumption made based on historical performances and it can change anytime when there is a market fluctuation. This means that despite investing in a stock that is profitable at the time, you could end up losing all your money.

Investing in a dividend-paying stock comes with its own set of perks. A dividend can act as a guaranteed return on the investment that you are making. Unlike regular stocks, you will receive a specific amount of dividend in the form of money or additional stocks at periodic intervals. This helps you make more profits out of your existing investment. Moreover, unlike bonds that have fixed rates of return throughout their life, dividend rates usually increase over time. It is highly unlikely that dividend-paying stocks will ever stop distributing dividends so once you invest in a suitable stock, you can expect to earn dividends for as long as you wish to hold the shares. The amount of dividend increases over time and you get to grow your investments. Sometimes, such growth can even be exponential.

When companies consistently pay dividends, it makes their stock more attractive to other investors in the long run. This in turn increases the stock prices because there is a sense of good reputation attached to the company and its policies. Apart from offering rewards, dividends also help in growing the value of stocks over time which attracts more investors and retains the old ones.

## *Equity Valuation*

Dividends play a very important role in the equity valuation of various companies. Equity valuation is a comprehensive technique used by analysts to find out the value of a company's equity. Some of the common tools used in equity valuation include fundamental analysis and technical analysis. Most analysts agree that evaluating equity based on dividends is much more reliable in comparison to other financial metrics like the price-earnings ratio and growth ratio (Maverick, 2021). This is because other metrics service their figures from the financial statements of the companies. These metrics are highly dependent upon the figures that have been provided by the company itself. If there is any manipulation of these figures from the company's side (which is very common), the results will become inconclusive. On the other hand, if you evaluate the dividend payments made by the company, you will be able to figure out the "real" position of the cash flow. If a company does not have a comfortable positive cash flow, it would never be able to distribute dividends. However, it is important to note here that companies often try to mask many problems and boost their reputation by increasing dividends. That is why you must be careful while considering dividends as an indicator of equity value. Although fundamental analysis can reveal this issue, it is best to be safe.

In comparison to other metrics, dividends provide conclusive proof of the financial health of the company. Companies usually revise dividend rates every year which means investors and analysts can easily determine a year-on-year dividend growth rate that can be indicative of the company's performance. Moreover, an annual rate change also provides a stable backdrop against which such analysis can be conducted. Unlike stock prices that change every day, evaluating dividends is much easier.

## Reduction of Risk

As we mentioned before, dividends act as a steady return on your equity stocks which in turn reduces the risk associated with stock market investments. However, the role of dividends as a hedge against market risk goes much beyond this one factor. Dividend-paying stocks tend to be more stable and studies have shown that these stocks have historically outperformed non-dividend-paying stocks in bear market periods (Maverick, 2021). When there is an overall downward market fluctuation, all kinds of stocks tend to reduce in value. However, most of the time it has been seen that the rate of decline in dividend-paying stocks is significantly lower than in other stocks. This can be attributed to the fact that companies that pay regular dividends are financially more solid and have the cash flow to handle a crisis better.

Although there has been a slight change in this trend in the recent COVID-19 pandemic-induced bear market, the fact remains that dividend-paying stocks outperform their non-dividend-paying counterparts. This is another reason why it is a good idea to start investing in these stocks because they have the potential to save you during a major financial downturn. You can rely on these returns in both good and bad times.

## Tax Benefits

Dividends generate additional income for the shareholder which is why they have tax implications as well. However, unlike other forms of income, dividends can offer you significant tax advantages. Qualified dividends are taxed at lower rates in comparison to ordinary income (O'Shea & Lam-Balfour, 2022). People who belong to the highest tax brackets pay only 20% of taxes on dividend income while people belonging to the lowest tax brackets are exempt from paying taxes on dividends (Maverick, 2021). When you earn dividends on stocks, you enjoy these tax benefits which can be a significant boost for the investor community.

*Purchasing Power*

Most investors do not realize the huge role that dividends play in preserving the purchasing power of capital. With inflation rates skyrocketing, an investment must fetch returns at a rate that is higher than the prevailing inflation rates. That is where dividends bring a difference to the table. Consider the following example.

You have purchased a stock of ABC Inc and the value of the stock grew 5% over the course of a year. However, the prevalent inflation rate in your country is 7% which means that despite your investment making a "profit," you are actually at a loss. If the stock you purchased pays a dividend of 3%, then you can retain your purchasing power and receive a net positive return on your investment.

## Choosing the Best Dividend Stocks

Not all companies pay dividends and before you start selecting stocks, you should be able to identify the ones that do. When companies pay dividends to their shareholders, it is a clear indication that the company is doing well financially, and they wish to reward its investors for being a part of the company. Since many companies have a long history of paying dividends to their shareholders, it is important to choose the right ones that would be beneficial for you. Here are a few steps that you can follow to choose the highest dividend-paying stocks.

- **Profitability in the Long Haul:** While choosing a dividend-paying stock, you should consider the long-term growth prospects of the company. Usually, a company having an annual growth rate between 5% to 15% is ideal if you want to purchase its dividend-paying stock (Bloomenthal, 2022). This is because this range exhibits stability and a growth rate above 15% can cause disappointment in earnings which in turn destabilizes the stock price. A company that grows gradually over time will keep on paying dividends to its shareholders at a consistent rate.

- **Cash Flow:** A stable cash flow is one of the greatest indicators of a well-balanced company. If you wish to choose a stock that pays high dividends, you should look for a company that has a good track record of paying dividends to its shareholders for at least five years. This consistent record can be regarded as a sign of the company's healthy cash flow and ability to pay dividends. It is important to have a working knowledge of the finances of a company before you start your dividend investing journey.

- **Consider Debt:** Before you invest in any stock, you must always check out the balance of the company to get an idea about its financial situation. A company that has a lot of debt but is still paying dividends to its shareholders is not in a good financial situation. You should avoid these companies when you choose dividend-paying stocks for your portfolio. Debt can play a major role in reducing the stock price of a company in the long run which is why you should be careful about it. The debt-equity ratio can be a good indicator to understand the financial condition and the burden of debt on a company's finances. A debt-equity ratio higher than two is unfavorable for any company.

- **Consider the Trends:** Apart from evaluating the individual company's performance over time, you should also check out the trends in the industry to which it belongs. Before you commit to investing in a stock, you must understand whether that industry will remain profitable for a long time.

    For example, historically it has been seen that stocks of soft drink companies are a safe bet because they always make good money for their shareholders. However, today's generation has become extremely conscious about their health which is why many of them are switching to healthier alternatives. That is why investing in a soft-drink company's stock might not be very profitable in the long run. (Bloomenthal, 2022)

    Dividend-paying trends can change over time and that is why you have to carefully consider the future of the industry in which you are investing. It is not always easy to understand what the future holds. However, with careful research and evaluation of important points, you can gain insight into which industries might be at risk of becoming obsolete.

Systematic investments into the stock markets over time can increase your chances of earning more dividends. Instead of considering them as "free gifts" from the company, you should seriously think about investing them and increasing your wealth. In the subsequent chapters, we will delve deeper into dividend investing and related concepts.

Chapter 2:

# Dividend Investing: The Beginning

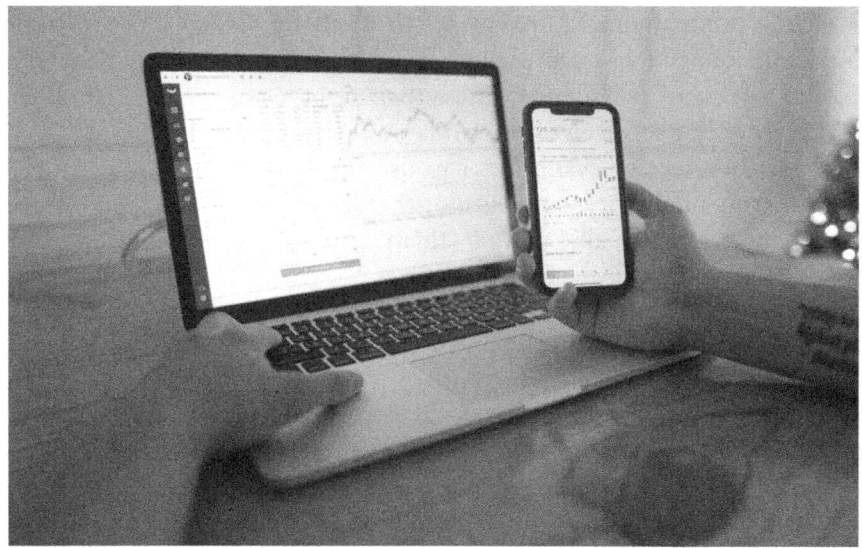

It has often been said that dividend stocks are only suitable for retired people who want to generate steady income and do not care for capital appreciation. However, that is not at all true! With the help of dividend investing, you can easily convert your dividend stocks into profitable growth investments that will help you to generate income and enhance your investment portfolio. In this chapter, we will begin our discussion about the fascinating concept of dividend investing and explain the various benefits and implications of the same.

## Understanding Dividend Investing

Dividend investing is the process of buying dividend-paying stocks and then investing the dividends received from them to buy additional units of the same stock or increase the value of your portfolio by making other investments. Apart from providing a steady income stream, dividend investing helps in enhancing your portfolio and contributes to growth (Kennon, 2022).

## *How Does Dividend Investing Work?*

Usually, a company makes payments to its shareholders in the form of dividends when they have earned enough profits to do so. They can also choose to pay dividends out of their reserves or retained earnings. A shareholder can receive dividends in cash or as additional units of stock. If they receive cash, they can use the same to buy more stocks and subsequently increase the size of their portfolio. When they receive stock, they are actually getting them for free which means their portfolio automatically gets a boost.

Consider the following example. You own four shares in XYZ Inc and each share costs $200. The company decided to pay 5% dividends which means you would receive a dividend of $10 per share you hold. In total, you receive a dividend of $40 per quarter which comes to around $160 in a year. As you keep increasing the number of shares you hold, your amount of dividend also increases. When you use these dividends to buy more shares, you are getting these additional shares for free. Over time, the value of dividend-paying stocks increases and after a few years, you will be left with shares worth thousands of dollars.

Instead of doing this process yourself, you can also find out if the company whose shares you own offers DRIPs. DRIPs are great ways to ensure that you are not losing out any money on the share prices because they help you to convert your cash dividends to new units of shares. Most companies offer DRIPs to their shareholders and it is a great and efficient way to increase your capital. However, you are not obligated to use DRIPs for collecting your dividends and you can choose to take the cash instead. DRIPs can be very helpful when you do not own many shares and the amount of cash that you are receiving is very small. Instead of taking $5 cash, if you can convert it to shares, you will be able to accumulate multiple additional units over the years.

## *Is Dividend Investing Safe?*

To answer this question, we have to consider the safety levels of dividends in general. Companies that regularly pay dividends belong to the most elite category. This is because a company needs to have solid financial health to keep on paying dividends. Moreover, dividends are usually paid out of profits, either current or past. When companies are paying regular dividends, it means that they are doing well in their business. Most stocks increase their dividend rates over the years which is also a good indication. If you are not sure about the company and the dividends it is paying, you can easily look up the details related to its earnings and profitability.

The financial details of all publicly-traded companies are available online and all you need to do is go through their website and look at the figures that you need for analysis. You should look at the profit figures and the dividend history to understand how the company is doing and whether they have a proven track record of paying dividends. Once you choose the right company, dividend investing is one of the safest ways to increase the value of your portfolio. You will receive the dividends at regular frequencies and all you need to do is make more investments with the money you receive or use DRIPs to convert the cash into additional units of stock. The main trick is to select the stock properly and for that, you have to conduct extensive research.

# Key Metrics to Understand Dividend Investing

Dividend investing can often be complicated because it involves the evaluation of a lot of factors. To understand the concept clearly, there are a few important metrics that you must know about. Please note that you do not have to physically calculate anything while you evaluate stocks or dividends. All of these metrics are easily available in most of the popular stock analysis tools that are commonly used by investors and brokers. It is important to simply understand the logic behind these ratios and why they are important. This will help you in making better investment decisions when you actually start your journey on dividend investing.

**Dividend Yield Ratio**

This is one of the most common metrics of dividend investing and is calculated as the ratio between dividends and stock price. For example, if a company pays $35 dividends annually and the current stock price is $750, then the dividend yield would be 35/750 = 4.7%. Although this is a fundamental metric, it cannot be used in isolation and it works well when you combine it with other dividend investing ratios. The dividend yield is also not the most stable metric because it can suddenly increase or decrease with dramatic fluctuations in the share price. If there is a decrease in stock price due to an internal conflict in the company, then the dividend yield will be higher even though it is not a representation of higher dividend payouts (Mohan, 2021).

**Dividend Payout Ratio**

This is a ratio between the dividend paid by the company and the net earnings earned by it in a certain accounting period. A very high dividend payout ratio is a good indication that there will not be any problems even if there is a downward market fluctuation. On the other hand, if the dividend payout ratio is very low and moves around zero, then you should think twice before buying the stock because it might not be dividend-paying. The dividend payout ratio varies between accounting periods because the figure of net income is usually taken from the financial statements prepared by the company.

**Monthly Dividend Income**

As a dividend investor, it is essential for you to track your income from your dividends regularly to determine how much you are earning and how your dividends are growing. The best way to do this is by tracking your monthly income from your dividends. You can use any online tool to filter out your monthly income or simply calculate the total dividend income received from a stock in a year and then divide the figure by 12. For example, if you have received $150 per quarter as dividends from a stock, then your annual income would be $600 and your monthly income would be $600/12= $50.

## Cost Base of DRIPs

Most companies offer DRIPs to their investors to convert the dividend that they have earned into more shares of the same stock. As mentioned before, it is a great way to increase your earnings and grow your capital over time. However, it is important to keep a track of the cost base that is used by DRIPs to make sure the price at which the new stocks are being acquired. The cost base is the price that the DRIPs are considering for acquiring the additional units with the dividend that has been earned by the investor. Since the prices are continuously fluctuating, it is important to ensure that you are not losing any value in procuring new units.

## Franking Credits

Countries like Australia have dividend imputation tax credits which are also known as franking credits (Mohan, 2021). With the help of these franking credits, an individual investor can claim a tax credit on their dividend income because the company has already paid taxes on their profits. This is a very effective way for the individual taxpayer to save money on taxes in the event the tax rate is very high on the earned dividends. Many times, the taxes paid by the company is more than the tax rate of the individual and in such cases, they will receive refunds from the tax authorities.

## Total Annualized Return

Total annualized return is not exclusively related to dividend investing. However, it provides an exhaustive insight into the dividend investing process and helps investors to understand how much they are earning from their investments. Usually, the total annualized return consists of elements like capital gains, dividends, currency fluctuations, brokerage, and time value of money (Mohan, 2021). It is used widely by all portfolio managers and investors to understand the health of their investments and the overall performance of their portfolios. Total annualized return is calculated as a ratio between the amount of return received and the amount invested and is influenced by all the elements mentioned above.

# Strategies for Dividend Investing

Most dividend investing strategies revolve around the concepts of either dividend yield or dividend growth. Although we will discuss these concepts in more detail in the subsequent chapters, let us have a quick overview of what they are.

- If you are looking for a high dividend yield, you can receive an immediate income in the form of cash payments. Usually, companies that have a large and steady cash flow are able to provide high amounts of dividends to their shareholders. As an investor, if you wish to generate income from your stocks immediately, then you can consider a stock that has a high dividend yield.

- The dividend growth principle is targeted at companies that do not pay large dividends but show significant growth in terms of their operation. In such a case, you would be buying more stocks of the company from the dividends that you are receiving to increase your equity holding. If you continue to invest these dividends and buy more stocks, after a few years, you can be holding a lot of stocks in a potentially well-established company. Over time, the value of the stock will also increase and contribute to capital appreciation.

Both of these strategies have their own sets of pros and cons and it usually depends on the risk appetite and time horizon of the investor as they make their choice.

# Does Dividend Investing Help You with Your Taxes?

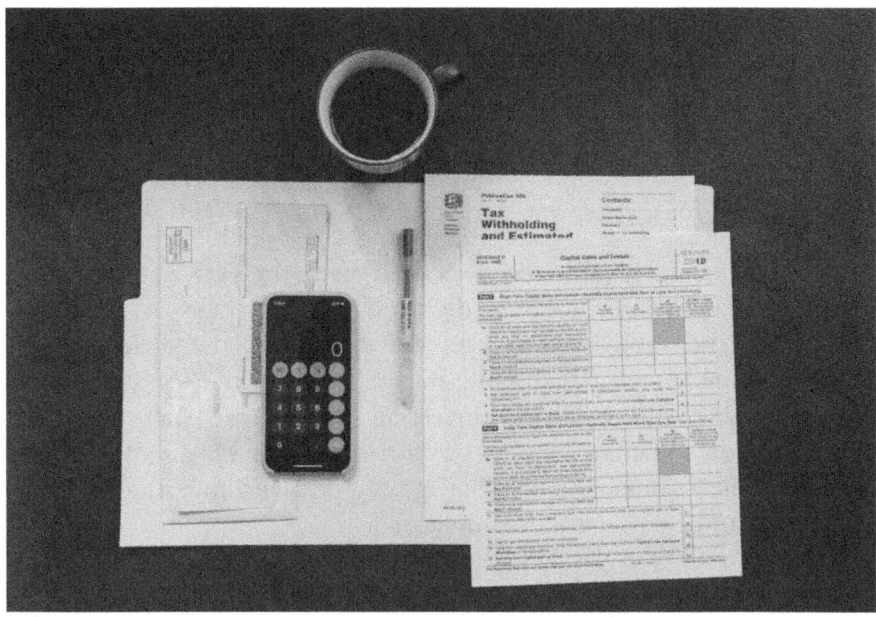

Dividend investing can help investors with tax benefits. If you are holding qualified dividends, then you will be paying capital gains taxes at much lower rates than ordinary rates of income tax. In fact, if you belong to lower tax brackets, you can get away with paying no taxes on your dividend income. If you receive dividends on your 401(k) or IRAs, you will not be eligible to pay any taxes on them until you withdraw the same. Dividend investing is a great way to save up on your taxes which leads to more income for you.

# Challenges of Dividend Investing (and How to Overcome Them)

Although dividend investing sounds like the most convenient investing strategy, it suffers from the following serious limitations. Let us look at the different problems associated with dividend investing and how you can work around them.

**Problem #1**

There is a lot of paperwork associated with the dividend investing process. If you are holding dividend-paying stocks of multiple companies, then you have to keep track of when the dividends are being announced, what is the present rate, and other necessary details to ensure that the dividend investing process is being executed properly. For someone who is not financially savvy, all of this can become quite overwhelming. That is why dividend investing is often considered to be tedious and complicated.

**Solution:** The best way to keep track of all these announcements is to hire a professional who will help you with it. If you don't want to hire someone, you have to set up a system that will help you plan and manage the paperwork. Many websites and apps help you to track the details of the stocks that you are holding.

**Problem #2**

After the expiry of the ex-dividend date, the price of the stock usually falls because the overall valuation of the stocks falls once dividends have been paid. This creates a negative impact in terms of capital appreciation and many investors panic because they feel their investment is losing its value. Many investors cash out their entire investments because of this drop in stock price and this creates a negative air around dividends and dividend investing.

**Solution:** As a long-term investor, you have to understand that falling stock prices after dividend distribution is a common phenomenon.

You cannot let yourself be carried away by something that is absolutely normal. It is almost like freaking out every time there is a big wave at the beach. Take time to choose the right stock and be patient as the stock regains its value after the dividend dates. Dividend-paying companies have a good reputation and they will bounce back after a few days.

**Problem #3**

Many investors conduct their investments through margin accounts. As a result, the brokers often take the shares of the stocks you own to lend them to other traders to wish to assume the short position for the stock (Kennon, 2022). This leads to a loss of dividends for these stocks because you are not really holding the stocks at the time.

**Solution:** Use a savings account to avoid this problem completely. You can also choose not to allow such activities on these accounts because it leads to higher taxes. When you lose the dividends, the broker pays you cash that is equivalent to the amount of dividend that you would have received. When money is credited to your margin account, it is treated as ordinary income and is taxed at higher rates. On the other hand, if you would have received a dividend, you could pay capital gain taxes on the same at lower rates.

By now, you must have gained clarity about the concept of dividend investing. They are not just additional payouts that you receive from the company. If you want to be skilled at dividend investing, you must take them seriously and consider them as viable investment units. In this context, it is important to understand that dividend growth is one of the most essential things that you need to remember while you are thinking of investing in them. In the next chapter, we will talk about various dividend models and how they help in evaluating dividend growth.

Chapter 3:

# Dividend Models

Now that you have a basic idea about how dividend investing works, it is time to delve into the technical part of the concept. There are various models that calculate dividend growth and earnings that consider a variety of factors. Although you will not be required to use these models and make the calculations yourself, their knowledge will help you gain clarity about the different concepts of dividend growth investing. It is very important to understand how these models work because once you start dividend investing, they will help you make suitable decisions according to your priorities.

## Dividend Growth Model

The main purpose of the dividend growth model is to compute the fair value of any stock. To do so, it uses the value of dividends that have been distributed by the stock in the past. There are usually two assumptions in this case:

- Dividends can keep on growing till perpetuity at a constant rate.

- Dividends can grow at a changing rate during a given period.

This model tries to establish a relationship between the fair value of a company's stock price, the current dividend of the company, and the rate at which it will grow in the future (Price, 2022). It is expressed as the following mathematical formula:

*Price = Current annual dividend ÷ (Desired rate of return-Expected rate of dividend growth)*

This formula is very helpful for dividend investors, especially when they are trying to figure out the viability of purchasing a stock. Usually, the historical growth rate is often considered the standard for calculating the future growth rate of dividends.

In the real world, a more complicated model is used for calculating the fair value of the stocks where different growth rates are used for different periods. Then the value of the dividends is discounted using a relevant discounting factor. This method helps in calculating the present value of future dividends. The assumption for these calculations is that the dividends grow at different rates in the initial periods after which the growth rate becomes constant and continues till eternity.

## Gordon Growth Model

The Gordon Growth Model assumes that dividends will continue to grow at a constant rate. It is calculated with the help of the following formula:

*P = D1 ÷ (r - g), where*

$P$ = *Currency price of the stock*

$D1$ = *Last paid dividend*

$r$ = *Required rate of return*

$g$ = *Constant growth rate that will continue till perpetuity*

Let us understand the model with a simple numerical example.

The stock of XYZ Inc is currently trading at $98.70. An investor wants to understand the intrinsic value of the stock to determine whether it is overvalued or undervalued. XYC Inc pays dividends to its stockholders. The present annual dividend is $7 while the required rate of return happens to be 14.75%. The dividends are expected to grow at the rate of 4% forever.

In this case, the fair value of the stock can be calculated in the following way:

$7 \div (14.75\% - 4\%) = \$65.12$

It is found that the fair value of the stock is lower than the current trading price. This means that the stock is overvalued and the investor should not purchase the same. On the other hand, if the investor is already holding units of stocks, then they should consider selling the same for making a good profit.

The biggest limitation of this model is that it assumes that growth rates are constant when in reality, we can find that this is never the case. Moreover, while calculating the intrinsic value of stocks, it has also been found that the growth rate can be greater than the required rate of return. Given the formula, the entire calculation would become invalid if that happened.

It is a simple model which is more suitable for theoretical calculations. Despite the limitations, it is still widely used by people to understand the over or undervaluation of dividend-paying stocks. Financial economics suggests that to achieve a state of equilibrium, the intrinsic value of a stock must be equal to its price.

If the intrinsic value is greater than the actual price of the stock, it means that the stock is undervalued. It can be a good opportunity for investors to buy more units of the stock because its price will definitely increase in the future and become equal to its intrinsic value. On the other hand, if the intrinsic value is lower than the price, it means that the stock is overvalued and it will soon fall to maintain financial equilibrium.

Dividend growth is one of the most important concepts in the context of dividend investing. The logic behind it is that over time, dividends will keep on growing and help in improving the overall condition of your portfolio. In fact, dividend growth is the major reason why people get involved in dividend investing. Apart from providing profits in the short run, dividend growth ensures that the investor receives adequate compensation in the long run as well.

However, the dividend discounting model is more popular in finding out the correct value of dividends and subsequently the value of the respective stocks. The dividend discount model has emerged to be more popular among investors especially who are interested in dividend investing strategies. This model is more close to the actual market conditions that analysts face while valuing stocks in the real world.

## Calculation of Dividend Growth Rate

According to financial expert James Chen (2020), "The dividend growth rate is the annualized percentage rate of growth that a particular stock's dividend undergoes over a period of time. Many mature companies seek to increase the dividends paid to their investors on a regular basis. Knowing the dividend growth rate is a key input for stock valuation models known as dividend discount models." Calculating the dividend growth rate is essential to understand how much dividend income a stock is capable of generating. It can be done using an arithmetic mean or a compound growth rate.

**Calculation Using Arithmetic Mean**

To calculate dividend growth rate using an arithmetic mean, the following formula is used (Srivastav, 2019):

$Gi = (G1 + G2 + ....... + Gn) / n$

Where *Gi= Target Growth Rate* and *G1= Dividend growth in a year*, and *n= Number of periods*.

Let us understand the calculation with the help of a simple numerical example. Consider the following dividends per share of stock for five years.

| Year | Dividend Per Share (in $) | Dividend Growth (%) |
|---|---|---|
| 1 | 5.75 | - |
| 2 | 6.89 | (6.89 - 5.75)/5.75 = 19.83 |
| 3 | 7.52 | (7.52 - 6.89)/6.89 = 9.14 |
| 4 | 8.39 | (8.39 - 7.52)/7.52 = 11.57 |
| 5 | 9.75 | (9.75 - 8.39)/8.39 = 16.21 |

Here, the number of periods would be four since we cannot consider the comparison in the first year.

$Gi = (G1 + G2 + \ldots\ldots + Gn) / n$

$Gi = (19.83 + 9.14 + 11.57 + 16.21)/4 = 14.1875\%$

## Calculation Using Compound Growth Rate

Consider the same data set as above.

| Year | Dividend Per Share (in $) |
|---|---|
| 1 | 5.75 |
| 2 | 6.89 |
| 3 | 7.52 |
| 4 | 8.39 |
| 5 | 9.75 |

The formula for compound growth rate is as follows (Srivastav, 2019):

$Gi = (Dn / D0)^{1/n} - 1$

Where $Dn$ = *Final Dividend*, $Do$ = *Initial Dividend*, and $n$ = *Number of periods*

So, $Gi = [(D5/D1)^{1/4}] - 1, = [(9.75/5.75)^{1/4}] - 1 = 14.11\%$

These calculations will give you an insight into how growth rate is calculated in dividend stocks. It is an important indication and helps dividend growth investors tremendously. We will discuss the details of dividend growth investing in the next chapter.

# Dividend Discounting Model

Before we discuss the dividend discounting model, let us first understand what discounting means. According to financial expert James Chen (2019), "Discounting is the process of determining the present value of a payment or a stream of payments that is to be received in the future. Given the time value of money, a dollar is worth more today than it would be worth tomorrow. Discounting is the primary factor used in pricing a stream of tomorrow's cash flows."

While calculating future cash flows, it is very important to consider the time value of money to determine the future values accurately. The dividend discount model is based on this principle and attempts to calculate the value of a stock using discounting factors over the period.

## *What Is the Dividend Discounting Model?*

The dividend discount model (DDM) is an analytical financial analysis model that calculates the present value of a company's stock price by adding the discounted value of all the future dividends that it will pay over a specified period (Chen, 2022a). Since it considers the time value of money and other prevailing market conditions for dividend valuation, it has high levels of accuracy. After calculation through the DDM method is done, the fair value of the stock is compared with the current price. If the fair value is greater than the price, then the stock is undervalued and if the fair value is lesser then the stock is overvalued. Investors and analysts frequently use these comparisons to make purchase decisions and try to figure out which market position would be the most profitable.

Predicting future dividend rates can be a difficult task because of the changing market conditions. Even if a company has a long record of paying dividends, nobody can predict the future accurately which means there might be inconsistencies in the dividend rate. To mitigate this issue, one commonly used method is assuming that the dividends grow at a constant rate forever till perpetuity (Chen, 2022a). Many analysts also study past trends to figure out a suitable dividend growth rate which is then applied to come to a suitable conclusion.

The formula for DDM can be described as follows:

*Value of Stock = Dividend Per Share/ (Cost of Capital - Growth Rate of Dividend)*

Here, the cost of capital can be determined with the help of the Capital Asset Pricing Model which considers beta, expected returns, and risk-free market returns. The main trick in this model is to calculate the value of dividends per share, which is often done after careful consideration of various factors. For a simple model, analysts can choose a constant growth rate while for a complicated multi-period model, different growth rates are considered for the initial periods before it stabilizes and becomes constant. In complex calculations, a present value (PV) factor is used to determine the present value of the future cash flows (Chen, 2022a). This is usually calculated with the help of a discounting rate. However, for simpler calculations, the PV factor is often ignored.

Although these models might be slightly technical, it is very important to have a complete understanding of them. Dividend models will form the foundation for you to apply dividend growth investing in your portfolio. Most of the strategies around dividend investing revolve around dividend yield and dividend growth. In the next chapter, we will have a detailed discussion about these two concepts so that you can figure out for yourself which one is more suitable for you.

Chapter 4:

# Dividend Growth Investing

Dividends can be a great source of generating investment returns if you are putting your money in the right stocks. They grow over time and help you to create a valuable portfolio. Dividend investors are often torn between the two concepts of dividend yield and dividend growth. Although yield provides us with a large income in the present period, dividend growth is what we should be aiming at. In this chapter, we will delve deeper into the concepts of dividend growth and yield so that you can understand the significance of each and figure out which strategy is more suitable for you.

## What Does Dividend Growth Investing Mean?

Dividend growth investing targets the growth elements in the dividends that you are earning. Since the size of the markets is continuously increasing, it is a general assumption that returns will increase over time. Dividend growth investors try to capture this growth and use it to increase the value of their portfolio. The most common way to do this is by reinvesting the cash received to buy additional units of the same stock or other high-paying stocks. Investors can use DRIPs to easily convert their cash into shares of the same stock. Many investors like to spice it up and use the cash for other high-return stocks as well. This enables them to buy newer stocks without paying any money. Dividend growth investing can be a very lucrative scheme for investors if they choose the right stocks.

### *How to Choose the Right Growth Stocks?*

Choosing the correct stocks for dividend growth investing can be a daunting task. It will involve extensive research about the history of companies and their dividend growth rate. In this process, you might find that many companies have a great overall growth rate in terms of valuation and profitability, but their dividends have not really grown over time. If you are aiming for dividend growth investments, you should steer clear of these companies. To conduct such research accurately, you have to understand the basics of calculating dividend growth rates, which we have already discussed in the previous chapter.

## *Dividends Are Great Indicators of Returns*

Most new investors tend to discard the impact of dividends as a part of their total returns. However, as a dividend growth investor, you must understand the role that dividends play in the total returns earned from a stock. According to a study on the impact of dividends on S & P 500 Funds published by Hartford funds, it was found that from December 1960 through December 2018, 82% of the index's total return consisted of dividends that were reinvested along with its compounding value that accrued during this period (Farrington, 2019).

This is conclusive proof that dividends contribute heavily to the total returns generated by the stocks. The effect of dividends is further understood when we factor in the growth component in these calculations. That is why dividend growth investing is of utmost significance in all economic conditions. Investors do not appreciate how dividends and their periodic growth can significantly boost their portfolios.

## *Limitations of Dividend Growth Investing*

If you have decided that you want to become a dividend growth investor, it is very important for you to understand the following limitations that it has.

- Even if you make all the right predictions, markets can surprise you by taking an unpredictable turn. Nothing is guaranteed in the financial markets and that is why dividend growth investing can be very volatile. For example, your entire investment plan might be based on a historical growth rate and due to certain internal inconsistencies, the company can decide to reduce its dividends. Then your growth calculations will become irrelevant and you might have to redo your entire plan.
- Dividend growth investing is strictly for the long term. You might have to wait for a long time, sometimes even decades before you can even understand the progress of your dividend

investing strategies. If an investor has a smaller time horizon, these strategies will not be suitable for them. For instance, day traders will not find it appealing to engage in dividend growth investing.

It will take a lot of patience and research to execute dividend investing correctly, which is why you should be sure that you want to do this.

## Dividend Yield Vs. Dividend Growth

Dividend investors are highly divided in their opinion when it comes to dividend yield and dividend growth. Usually, yield is more concerned with the short term while growth accumulates in the long term. However, this is an oversimplification of the entire concept and there should be more explanation about the same. There can be an argument that the choice of dividend yield or growth in dividend investing depends on the time horizon but ultimately it depends on the choice of the individual investors. Both options can provide the desired results if executed properly.

## *What Is Dividend Yield?*

We have already talked about the calculation of the dividend yield ratio. The concept of dividend yield refers to the number of dividend earnings that a stock is providing in a given period. Usually, it is represented in an annualized format which is calculated by multiplying the quarterly dividend rates by four. For example, if the dividend per share (annualized) is $7.25 and the price of the share is $91, then the dividend yield is 7.25/91 or 7.97%. The dividend yield is usually expressed as a percentage of the stock price.

Although it is widely used by investors, the dividend yield is not always a great indicator of how the stock is doing. In fact, it does not even provide a proper representation of the dividends that are being distributed. Consider the following example.

AB Inc pays an annualized dividend of $12 per share and it has a share price of $96 at the end of an accounting year. The annual dividend yield in this case is 12%. During the next year, the company ran into some internal problems regarding its supply chain management and ended up losing an entire unit of its operations. This resulted in the reduction of the stock price from $96 to $84. The company decided to keep the dividends the same because it did not want to lose its investor base. So, assuming they kept their annualized dividend at $12 per share, their dividend yield would now increase to around 14.23%. Although this is an increase from the previous 12%, if you look at the situation carefully, you will find that such an increase is not an indicator of the improvement of the financial health of the company or its dividend-paying capacity.

This example is just a testimony to the fact that dividend yields do not always show the correct positions of dividends and stocks. It should not be used by investors as the sole metric based on which they make their dividend investing decisions. Many sectors like utilities have high dividend yields because they have a stable financial condition and keep increasing their dividends every year. The rate of increase in dividend yield can be understood clearly for these companies. However, most stocks present a somewhat unclear picture of their dividend yield because of the constant price movements. There is no way you will ever be able to come to a distinct conclusion by only using dividend yields.

Investors must understand that dividend yield is only good when you are just concerned with the income that you are receiving from your stocks. However, that should not be your only goal. Dividends have immense growth potential and unless you factor such growth into your investment decisions, you will not be doing justice to your portfolio. Dividend yield should be used in combination with growth strategies to truly reap their benefits. While yield will help you in determining your current income, growth metrics will assist you in understanding how you can use such income to create long-term wealth. Both of these elements have significance in a dividend investing strategy.

## What Is Dividend Growth?

Dividend growth is the concept where we use a growth rate to understand how the dividends have been increasing or decreasing over time. Most companies that have a proven track record of paying regular dividends have an increasing dividend growth rate. This is a great metric for dividend investors because dividend growth is what they must be aiming for in the long run. A company that shows consistent dividend growth has got great financial health and a solid cash flow because it is continuously dividing its profits among its shareholders. Most investors consider dividend growth to be suitable for people seeking passive income from their investments. However, dividend growth can be helpful for all categories of investors because the growth will ultimately help them in growing their portfolios.

For example, you are holding stocks in a company that pays regular dividends growing and increasing consistently. This means that you are receiving a steady stream of income from your equity investments. You are a relatively young investor and have a job that is your primary source of income and you are not dependent on the passive income from your dividends for your lifestyle. This presents a unique opportunity for you because you can use these dividends however you like. One obvious option is to use DRIPs and convert the dividends into additional shares of the same stock that you already hold. In this way, the total value of your portfolio will rise and you will be holding a larger portion of the equity of the company. Over time, when the company grows, your investments will also grow, enabling you to reap the benefits of dividend growth. This is the most common strategy for dividend growth investors and it requires very little effort from your end as an investor.

Now let us come to some of the more unconventional ways in which you can use dividends to grow your portfolio. Most investors are skeptical about putting their money in risky instruments because of the fear of loss. However, following the general rule of investing, riskier investments also tend to provide higher returns. To truly reap the benefits of market movements, you have to invest some of your money in these risky stocks especially if you are a relatively young investor. Using your hard-earned money might make you uncomfortable which is why there is another way. Start using your dividends to fund these risky investments.

For example, if you wish to invest in stocks of young technology companies or other asset classes like cryptocurrencies, you can use the cash you receive from your dividends. In this way, you are technically not spending any money to procure your risky investments and if you make a profit from them, then the entire amount is your gain because there is no cost of acquisition involved. Over time, the value of your dividend stocks will increase because it is a good company with solid financials. So by using the dividends to fund other investments, you can easily increase the overall value of your investment portfolio, without spending additional money.

## *Growth Is an Indication That the Operating Environment Is Healthy*

You should always consider growth as the more important determinant than yield. A company that is paying a high dividend per share today might not always be able to sustain itself in the long run. There have been numerous instances where companies that pay large dividends have failed to keep up their yield and then faced natural decline. While high yield is an attractive quality in a dividend stock, growth is the indicator of stability. If you look at it from a comprehensive viewpoint, growth shows that the operating environment of a company is healthy.

A company can have a high dividend yield ratio now. However, you have to consider the consistency factor before you invest in it. When you analyze the dividend growth of a company for a certain period, it shows that the company is consistently having high profits and is doing well in its business. Dividend yield can increase due to several reasons. Consider the example in the previous section where we talked about how the dividend yield of AB Inc increased because of a reduction in stock price. This is a very common real-life scenario which is why yield cannot be considered completely reliable. When dividends are growing, it means that the company is making the right decisions and their business is flourishing. This is an exhaustive indicator and must be given due importance especially when you are considering dividend investing.

In the long run, you should be targeting dividend growth above yield. This is because the ultimate objective of every investment portfolio is growth and capital appreciation. Profits in the short run might not be able to sustain you for life which is why you need to create provisions for the future. The best way to do it is dividend growth investing because growth accelerates the stocks and in turn boosts the performance of the company.

# Chapter 5:

# Dividend Growth Investing Strategies

The basic principle of investing is that you need to have a set of distinct strategies that will help you to navigate all market conditions and dividend growth investing is no exception. Although this is a very profitable investment option, most investors are still unaware of the nuances of dividend growth investing which is why you must have a set of strategies ready for yourself which will help you in better decision-making. In this chapter, we will discuss some of these strategies and assist you in understanding which one might be suitable for you. Please note that these strategies might not seem very customized to you and if you are unsure, it is always a good idea to consult a professional.

# Strategies to Follow

Here is a list of interesting strategies that you can follow when you decide to start dividend growth investing. These strategies are not exhaustive and there can be modifications to all of them.

**Strategy #1: Build a Collection of Shares**

The first and most important strategy is to invest in stocks of different companies that pay dividends at high rates. While choosing the stocks, make sure that the dividend yield is greater than the inflation rate because it will help you beat the overall expenses that you might have to incur along with your investments (Kennon, 2021). Beating the inflation rate is very important to ensure profits in the long run. You can truly get the benefit of dividend growth investing when you have a net gain right from the beginning. Given the current inflationary economic conditions, you might find it slightly difficult to find a high dividend rate, but thorough research is required to look for such stocks. You can start with stable companies (like utilities) that have a great history of financial health and regular dividend payments. It can be wise to select companies that have been around for at least a decade or so to increase your chances of creating a good portfolio.

Since we are in a high inflationary period, it is advisable to keep building a collection of shares, especially in energy, financials, REITS, or consumer staples companies. Companies that have been around for a long time have high market sustenance. Inflation will cause a temporary fall in prices and you should take advantage of the same.

**Strategy #2: Diversify**

In any investment portfolio, diversification is the best strategy that you can adopt, and dividend growth investing is no exception. Just like you have to create a collection of different stocks, you have to venture into different industries as well. This will help you in the event of any and every major market fluctuation. The diversification should also be cyclical, non-cyclical, and among different markets as well. For example, technology stocks tend to have high-profit margins, but they perform badly whenever there is an economic crisis. That is why you should include stocks of industries like utilities and pharma because they can give your portfolio much-needed stability.

## Strategy #3: Hold, Hold, and Then Keep on Holding

To truly reap the benefits of dividend investing, you have to wait for a long time. Sometimes, it can be decades before you can understand how your dividends are growing which is why holding your investments is going to be one of the most important strategies that you can follow. It might seem like a test of your patience, but holding your investments for a long time can actually help you get the benefits of deferred taxes (Kennon, 2021). You can get the benefit of capital appreciation and your next of kin will be rewarded with more dividends. Holding your investments is a great strategy for generating passive income in the long run. If you start investing in your 30s and continue till retirement, then the passive income from your dividends might just be enough to get you through your post-retirement years. Of course, it would depend on the amount of investment you are making but holding your dividend stocks can generate a lot of income for you over time.

## Strategy #4: Checking Company Financials Regularly

When people invest in a dividend-paying stock that has a great financial performance, they usually rely on the goodwill of the company and do not bother to stay updated about its affairs. As an informed investor, this should never be your attitude. Just because a company made a good impression on you initially, does not mean it will continue doing so. Don't be overwhelmed by the regular dividend payouts and increasing yields. You must be aware of the company policies and how they are paying the dividends. As you already know, dividends are paid out of current or past retained profits. If you find that the company is paying dividends out of debt, then it is not a good indication of its financial health and you should consider cashing out your investment while there is still some amount of stability left. With all the modern tools that are available right now, it is very easy to check all these documents. If you need help understanding them, consult a professional who can assist you. Always remember, it is okay to ask for help. Even if you did not hire a professional initially, you can decide to do so at any point in your investing journey.

## *Which Strategy Is Useful for You?*

There is no right strategy that goes for everyone. You have to choose the strategies that are suitable for you based on your risk tolerance level and financial priorities. Despite all the discussion, if you feel you are more concerned with short-term profits, then you can always go for the dividend yield approach. It can give you the income that you are looking for in the form of dividends and help you with tax benefits as well. You can always choose to sell your investments if you find the profits are not enough for you.

For comparatively longer-term investors, focus on growth should be of utmost importance. Since you are in it for a greater time horizon, you have the time to recover from any losses that you might incur due to market fluctuations. Make sure to revise your strategy from time to time so that it stays relevant to all the recent market trends.

These strategies will help you to determine your goals and fix up your priorities when you try dividend growth investing. However, it is important to note that only dividend growth investing will not help you to achieve all your investment goals and you need to have a well-balanced portfolio for that. In the next chapter, we will talk about portfolio management and its importance so that you know what you need to do to get the most out of your investments.

Chapter 6:

# Portfolio Management

Investing is a fascinating activity that can help you to grow your money multiple times over the years. When you choose the right kind of stocks and other instruments, you can earn huge profits. However, it is very important to create a selection of investments that can meet all your needs and this is where the concept of a portfolio comes into the picture. No matter the kind of investments you make, you have to understand the significance of creating a portfolio that will grow with you and protect you from market fluctuations. In this chapter, we will talk about the various elements of portfolio management and how you can prepare your portfolio according to your goals.

# What Is Portfolio Management?

Portfolio management can be regarded as the art and science of choosing investments according to the specific needs of an individual or institution that will help them to maximize their earnings in their specified time horizon (Hayes, 2019a). It is an important process that helps an investor to achieve their investment objectives and handle all kinds of market risk.

While many individuals manage their own portfolios, institutions or large investors like to hire licensed professionals for managing their portfolios because of the diverse needs that they have. A portfolio manager has to understand the priorities of their clients and make choices that include decisions related to risk-return trade-offs, debts, equities, growth, and stability (Hayes, 2019a).

Professionals usually use the following techniques to conduct portfolio management:

- **Asset Allocation:** Asset allocation is the process of allotting money to specific securities based on the financial priorities and risk appetite of the investors. This would include choosing stocks and other financial instruments that are both volatile and non-volatile so that the investor can expose themselves to a variety of market elements and earn profits in the process.

- **Diversification:** Diversification is the process of allocating money to different kinds of assets that would create a well-balanced portfolio. This helps the investor in earning profits while mitigating the risks related to stock market investments. It is an essential part of the portfolio management process and involves choosing securities from different industries and volatility levels.

- **Rebalancing:** The process of portfolio management is not static and needs to change along with changing market conditions. That is why portfolio rebalancing is an important part because it involves changing the asset allocations to ensure that the investor is getting a higher yield from their investments. Rebalancing helps to keep the portfolio relevant according to the requirements and market trends.

## *Process of Portfolio Management*

Portfolio management is a structural process that is conducted by professionals with a lot of precision to ensure the objectives of individual investors are being fulfilled. If you want to conduct portfolio management by yourself, it is important to understand how the process works. Here is a step-by-step guide to the process so that you can gain insight into the different procedures involved.

**Step 1: Identify Objectives**

The first step in creating and managing an investment portfolio is to identify the objectives of the individual investors. Usually, this can include receiving stable returns, achieving capital appreciation, or a mix of both. This is important because the rest of the steps will depend on what the investor actually wants from their investments. The clarity of these objectives is extremely critical. The investor must be sure about the percentage of growth, volatility, and the value of beta for any investment. The objectives here should be SMART: Specific, Measurable, Attainable, Realistic, and Time-bound (Corporate Finance Institute, 2022).

**Step 2: Estimate the Capital Market**

Every portfolio manager conducts a thorough analysis of the capital market before they start choosing investments. This includes evaluating the expected returns of each investment category and comparing it with the risk involved to execute the steps. If you are managing your own portfolio, this can be an important factor that will determine the success of your investments. Hence it is critical to have clarity on what is your overall expected return in your portfolio. There are various ways to evaluate this.

## Step 3: Decide How to Allocate Assets

Asset combinations are the most important elements of any investment portfolio. Depending on your risk appetite and investment goals, you have to select the allocation of assets that are suitable for you. For example, if you have a high-risk tolerance level, you can choose to invest heavily in equities that are risky but provide high returns and a little portion for fixed-income securities. If you have a lower risk tolerance, you may want to invest majorly in fixed-income securities and less in equities.

## Step 4: Formulate Strategies for Investing in Securities

Once a portfolio manager has chosen the appropriate securities, they will devise a suitable strategy for investing in them. This will depend on the investor's time horizon and the amount of money they want to invest at different intervals. For example, if you are looking to invest as a lump sum, your strategies will differ from someone else's who wishes to invest smaller amounts every month.

## Step 5: Select the Appropriate Investments

After careful consideration of the asset allocation and portfolio strategies, the portfolio managers choose the appropriate investments for their clients. This is done after careful market research and conducting fundamental and technical analyses of different categories of stocks. For people seeking regular income, high-performing dividend stocks are chosen that have a proven track record of great financial health.

## Step 6: The Most Important Step

Despite all the planning, this is the most important step. Putting your strategy into action.

## Implementing the Process

Finally, the manager would implement the process by actually investing in the selected stocks. This is done once the client has transferred the necessary funds required for investment. After you have defined your allocation and which equity to purchase, and your purchasing plan,

Technical Analysis can be a good tool to help you "when" to enter a position.

**Step 7: Evaluating and Revising the Portfolio**

After the investment, the manager usually evaluates the performance of the stocks to determine if they need to make any necessary revisions. This is often done to ensure that the stocks that they have chosen are actually performing the functions according to the financial priorities of the client. The same goes if you are managing the portfolio on your own. You must check if the key assumptions you had before purchasing your equities are still relevant or have totally changed over the past months or years.

**Step 8: Rebalancing**

Periodic portfolio rebalancing is an important part of the management process. In this phase, the manager determines if they need to make shifts to other stocks or move funds from one stock to another.

This process will help you to understand what you need to do to build a well-balanced investment portfolio. It is very important to revisit your portfolio in frequent intervals because the markets are dynamic and you have to keep up with the changing trends.

## *Active and Passive Portfolio Management*

Investors and portfolio managers use the following techniques for their investment portfolios.

- **Active Portfolio Management:** In active portfolio management, the manager deals with closed-end funds and tries to beat the performance of the index by actively buying and selling investments (Hayes, 2019a). In such cases, the portfolio is dynamic, and managers use different kinds of analytical techniques to ensure that the stocks they are choosing will yield the maximum results.

- **Passive Portfolio Management:** Passive portfolio management is synonymous with investing in index funds which is why it is also known as indexing or index investing (Hayes, 2019a). It is a suitable strategy for passive investors who wish to invest money for the long term and do not want to keep switching investments. The general notion is that index funds will grow over time which makes this strategy quite useful for investors with a big-time horizon.

## Risk Appetite and Risk Tolerance

While we are on the topic of investment portfolios, it is very important to have a conversation about risk appetite and risk tolerance. As an investor, you should have a clear idea about their meaning and what they entail so that you don't end up investing in something you are not comfortable with.

## What Is Risk Appetite?

Risk appetite is considered to be the amount of risk an organization or individual is ready to undertake to achieve its objectives (Shackleford, 2021). This is more valid on an organizational level and is dependent on the following factors:

- **The Culture:** Every organization has a distinct culture and risk appetite is part of their traditions. Many companies traditionally do not like to undertake risk while others have a risk-loving attitude. This is the same for individuals.

- **The Industry:** Based on the industry to which they belong, companies often have varying degrees of risk appetite.

- **Competitors:** If the competitors of an organization are undertaking risky endeavors, there might be general pressure to do the same.

- **Type of Objectives:** Many organizations and individuals have very high goals that require a lot of funds. To achieve such goals, it is often necessary to undertake a great degree of risk.

## What Is Risk Tolerance?

Risk tolerance is more granular in nature. It applies to individual investors rather than large institutions. A person might have a high-risk appetite but that does not always mean they will have a high-risk tolerance level. Even if their circumstances demand them to undertake more risk, they might not have the stomach to actually go through with it. Risk tolerance is a sensitive concept and depends on a lot of factors like the financial condition of the person in the present situation. For example, a person wants to quit their job after five years and wants to launch a startup. They understand that if they have to achieve this goal, they need to save aggressively and invest in high-return stocks which can be potentially risky. However, at the moment, they got married and had a child which put significant pressure on their finances. They are still able to invest the amount they were initially doing but given the circumstances, their risk tolerance level has been brought down.

## *Relationship Between Risk Appetite and Risk Tolerance*

The two are related and often risk tolerance takes the high seat in making investment decisions. Life is mostly concerned with what happens day-to-day, and if some situations are preventing you to take risks, then your risk tolerance is bound to act up and even override your risk appetite. As a rational investor, you have to understand your risk appetite and make decisions based on both risk appetite and risk tolerance.

# The Concept of Beta

When it comes to analyzing risk, beta is the most important indicator that is used by analysts all over the world. It is the determinant of risk and helps investors to understand how a stock is performing in comparison to the market.

According to Investopedia (2019), "The beta is the number that tells the investor how that stock acts compared to all other stocks, or at least in comparison to the stocks that comprise a relevant index." While evaluating the stock markets, we look at the movement of the entire index. For instance, the S & P 500 Index keeps on fluctuating daily but that does not give us the impression it casts on individual stocks (Investopedia, 2019). Beta helps us capture the sensitivity of a stock's price in comparison to the entire index. If the beta of Stock A is 0.80, it means that when the market index moves by one basis point, the value of Stock A will move 0.80 basis points in the same direction.

Beta helps in understanding a stock's volatility and making comparisons to the market index. The Greek letter 'ß' is used to denote it in financial mathematics.

## *Understanding Beta*

Beta is a complicated tool to measure risk and is usually calculated using statistical regression. However, as an individual investor, you do not have to delve into the details of such calculations. To understand and correctly interpret Beta, you have to understand the values it assumes and what they imply.

| Beta Value | Implication |
|---|---|
| Negative | Beta is usually not negative. A negative beta would indicate that the stock moves in an opposite direction from the market. This does not happen because stocks and the index tend to have the same trends. Real estate and gold might have negative beta because they perform well even when the market is falling but there is no conclusive evidence to establish the same. However, if you find any security that has a negative beta, you should consider investing in it because it will act as a hedge against market risk. |
| Zero | A security with zero beta means that it does not correlate with the market. This means that even if the market moves drastically, the value of the security will remain unchanged. Cash has a beta of zero because its value stays constant in all market conditions, provided there is no inflation (Investopedia, 2019). |
| Between Zero and One | The companies whose stocks have beta values between zero and one tend to be less volatile to market changes. For example, many utility companies fall into this category (Investopedia, 2019). Usually, companies that are stable and have consistent financial health have beta values between zero and one. |

| Beta Value | Implication |
| --- | --- |
| One | A stock that has a beta of one moves exactly like the market which means if the market moves by 2 basis points, it will do the same in that direction (Investopedia, 2019). Usually, index stocks have a beta of one. |
| Greater than One | Companies that are highly volatile have a beta greater than one. This means that they are moving at a higher rate than the market. Many young technology companies have a beta higher than one because of their swift movements and volatility (Investopedia, 2019). |
| Greater than 100 | If you see that the beta value of any stock is greater than 100, then it is probably a technical error. A stock that has such high volatility will lose all its value when the market moves even slightly in the negative direction. |

## *Importance of Beta*

Despite some of the inconsistencies in its calculation, beta is one of the most useful tools in evaluating risk and volatility. Risk-averse investors like to understand how their stock will move if there is a slight change in the markets. Beta gives a clear indication of how volatility works and it will be helpful for investors to compare it with their risk tolerance level. For example, a risk-averse person might prefer stocks that have a beta value between zero and one. On the other hand, a risk lover would look for higher beta stocks. Usually, established companies do not have a beta greater than four, but if somebody wants to play with some risky stocks to earn huge returns, they will invest in high-beta stocks (Investopedia, 2019).

## *Beta of Your Portfolio*

Portfolio beta is simply the weighted average beta of all stocks and securities that you own. Consider the following table.

| Stocks | Beta | Weight in the Portfolio | Weighted Average |
|---|---|---|---|
| A | 1.20 | 0.35 | 0.42 |
| B | 0.20 | 0.30 | 0.06 |
| C | 4.00 | 0.20 | 0.8 |
| D | 0.80 | 0.15 | 0.12 |
| Beta of the Portfolio | | | 1.40 |

However, before delving deeper into the analysis of beta, you must evaluate your own risk tolerance level. Beta can only be a helpful measure if you know what you want. The biggest trick of managing your portfolio lies in understanding your risk appetite and comparing it with your risk tolerance. It is absolutely fine if you are not comfortable with high-risk stocks. You should only invest in stocks that suit your priorities. Choose stable stocks that will provide you with dividends regularly which will help you to grow your income and promote capital appreciation. These stocks will usually have a beta value between zero and two.

## *Why You Should be Careful While Analyzing Beta*

Despite the many advantages of beta, there are certain things that you should consider while using it as an analysis tool.

- Beta uses historical data to show the pattern of a stock's volatility in comparison to the market. The entire process is based on past data and does not provide any details about future predictions. Although the past patterns provide accurate indications most of the time, there is never any guarantee of the same. Markets are dynamic and complicated and they can change at any time which can make beta values quite useless.

- Beta only considers systematic risk which pertains to the entire market index. Systematic risk is the risk that affects all the companies of a particular industry or all stocks in an index and is highly general in nature. Beta does not capture the impact of unsystematic risk which is particular to each company. Internal conflicts, policies, and other issues can often become a determining factor in changing stock prices and beta does not consider any of that. This makes it an inadequate measure of risk.

Portfolio management is the most essential part of your investing journey. If you can create a well-balanced portfolio that helps you to mitigate risks over time, then your investments will automatically grow and give you the profits you need. However, it is important to understand that portfolio management strategies have to change over time so that you can keep up with the changing situations. In the next chapter, we will talk about how you can prepare yourself and your investment for different times and the strategies that you need to follow to tackle a bear market.

Chapter 7:

# Investment Tips in Changing Situations

The COVID-19 Pandemic has taught us that the world can take a drastic turn at any time without any prior intimation. Apart from the social factors and medical emergencies, one of the biggest issues that took the world by storm was widespread economic distress. The stock markets began to underperform, inflation rates skyrocketed, and the entire world economy came to a standstill. The world was not prepared for such a catastrophic event. This was a good moment to reflect on your investment decisions and create a portfolio that would be "pandemic-proof." In this chapter, I will talk about how you can make necessary arrangements for your portfolio so that it can withstand adverse situations and continue to grow even during the worst phases of the economy.

## Some General Investment Tips

One of the best investment strategies that you can follow in every economic climate is to keep things simple. Do not overcomplicate your portfolio because it will come to bite you back when there is a financial crisis. Invest in stocks, securities, or commodities that you understand, and don't go for anything flashy. Always remember, your portfolio is not something that you have to show off to others. It should just make sense to you and help you to navigate your financial goals. One of the biggest mistakes that people make is that they try to imitate others while creating their investment portfolio. It doesn't work that way and you end up hurting yourself. The investment portfolio that you create for yourself should be tailored according to your needs and risk appetite. For instance, if you are in your late 40s and trying to build a retirement fund for yourself, cryptocurrencies should not be your choice of investment. Just because it is a highly hyped asset class, does not mean you should start putting all your money into it. You have to evaluate your needs and create a plan that will help you to grow your money and fulfill your financial requirements.

### *How Is Dividend Growth Investing Different?*

People have a misconception about dividend investing that they simply have to invest the extra income that they are earning. However, dividend growth investing truly reaps benefits when you increase the time horizon. Don't think about the benefits that you are getting now but what you can do with it after a few years.

The first step is always to choose the right dividend stocks carefully. In our previous book, *Dividend Investing for Beginners,* we have discussed in great detail how you can choose the best dividend-paying stocks. The most important thing is to choose a company that has a lower proportion of debt and has a proven track record of paying dividends for a long time. Although it may sound conflicting, a lower payout ratio is better for the investors because this means that the company is retaining a greater proportion of its profits that it can use to grow and pay further dividends.

As we have already mentioned, dividends play an important role in the overall growth of your portfolio and help you to get access to profits from different types of industries. Dividends provide a kind of stability to the stocks because the companies need to have a solid financial background to be able to pay dividends to their shareholders regularly. When you invest your dividends over time, you have the chance of creating a well-balanced portfolio that will be able to withstand different types of market adversities.

## *The Benefit of Compounding*

The biggest benefit of having a long time horizon is that you get to enjoy the fruits of compounding. The money keeps on increasing over time and you get great returns on your investments. While considering a long-term investment, make sure that you choose something that provides you with the necessary growth and stability.

When you choose a company for investing in, you must verify whether it can create value and distribute the same to its investors. A company needs to be making smart investments that help in its capital and dividend growth.

# Investing Strategies for a Bear Market

The recent COVID-19 pandemic brought about severe economic downturns and ushered in another bear market period. Bear markets are fairly common, and they occur frequently which is why you have to prepare yourself and your portfolio to withstand the same. A bear market is a period when the whole financial markets experience severe and prolonged fall in prices. It is a condition when the overall prices of securities fall more than 20% from the recent highs and there is a widespread negative attitude in the market that dampens investor spirits (Chen, 2019).

It is very important to have a distinct set of bear market investing strategies because we are living in times of severe economic uncertainties. Bear markets are characterized by reductions in prices and everyone is freaked out because they have no idea how they will handle such difficult times. The biggest thing that you can do to support yourself through this time is to keep calm and have a plan ready. In this section, we will talk about some of the popular bear market investing strategies that will help you to grow your portfolio even during times of economic crisis.

## *Don't Let Fear Take Over You*

Although this might sound like cliched advice, this is the first thing to remember when you are facing a bear market. Even if it seems catastrophic right now, chances are that these situations will not be anything more than a statistic a few years later. In the grand scheme of things, every crisis is small and you have to convince yourself that no matter how difficult it seems, it will pass. Stay calm and don't freak out because you will be hurting your chances of creating a growth portfolio. Panic makes people do the stupidest of things, so don't let yourself be carried away by fear.

## *Dollar Cost Averaging*

As an investor, you need to understand that the stock market will have its bad years. Recently, in an interview with CNN, Amazon founder Jeff Bezos asked people to keep their cash safe and requested American families to not spend money on big-ticket items like expensive television sets or refrigerators in the holiday season because the "economy does not look good right now" (Sukheja, 2022). These statements are an indication of an upcoming recession in the United States and have already sent fear signals to the whole world. Although this is valuable advice from a wise man, you should remember that these things keep happening in the economy.

When you are a long-term investor with a time horizon of more than a decade, then you should consider applying dollar cost averaging principles to your portfolio. Dollar-cost averaging is an investment strategy that helps people to deal with uncertain economic times by automating investment amounts (Chen, 2021). In this method, you will be investing a specific amount every month (or at any specific periodic intervals) and this will help in reducing the average cost of the investments over time, which in turn helps in lowering the effect of price volatility on your portfolio.

This is a great investing strategy for the long term because you do not have to worry about timing the market for specific prices. You can simply keep on investing as long as you want to and after a certain period, you will find that the investments have grown and you have averaged the price of the securities that you bought. The trick is to keep on buying, irrespective of the market conditions. It might sound unusual, but trust me, dollar cost averaging is one of the best bear market investing strategies that you can follow.

## *Play Dead*

The term "playing dead" stems from the fact that if you encounter a bear in a forest, the best strategy would be to act as if you are dead to ensure that the bear does not attack you. Here, the wild bear is a metaphor for the bear markets, and when there are widespread price reductions, staying calm and playing dead is a great strategy. As a part of this policy, you can choose to shift funds from the stock market to safer securities certificates of deposit (CDs), U.S. Treasury bills, and other highly liquid instruments that have shorter maturity periods (Investopedia, 2022).

## *Diversify According to Your Affordability*

Diversification is one of the most common investment strategies in any market condition because it helps in reducing market risk to a great extent. In a bear market, you should aim at diversification but make sure that you are doing it according to your affordability. You cannot be spending more than you should just because you want to include the elements of diversification in your portfolio.

## *Search for Values*

Bear markets can provide a great opportunity to buy more high-value stocks at a lower price (Investopedia, 2022). Whenever the economy enters a bear market period, the prices of all the stocks start declining. This means that you have the potential to procure blue chip stocks by paying much lower because the whole market has become undervalued. Instead of panicking, you should consider the bear markets to be the time to start investing and searching for value stocks. However, you should remember to invest within your affordability range.

## *Search for Defensive Industries*

Even when the world has entered into a full-fledged recession, certain items will not see a dip in sales. Household non-durables like toothpaste, shaving cream, and shampoo are examples of defensive industries that will continue to flourish in bear markets, and you should consider investing in these stocks to create a hedge against the market risk (Investopedia, 2022).

## *Include Some Cash*

Investors often tend to ignore the potential of cash as a long-term investment because of the long returns. However, during times of economic crisis, cash can be one of the most useful assets because it offers you a great deal of diversification. Moreover, cash is an independent asset class which means that it has a very low correlation with other assets. It is not easily affected by market volatilities, and it can help you mitigate the overall risk associated with bear markets.

## *Find a Financial Consultant*

The best thing to do in times of any financial crisis is to find a professional who can guide you according to your requirements. Even if you gather a ton of knowledge about the various aspects of investing, the knowledge that a professional has is unparalleled and you should consider seeking their help to ease your burdens.

The biggest thing that you should learn about bear markets is that they don't last very long. You have to wait till things are better.

As we come to the end of the book, let me share a secret with you. No matter how many strategies you devise and the right steps you take, your investment portfolio is bound to suffer when there is a major economic crisis. When the whole world is suffering financially, your portfolio will suffer losses too and there is nothing you can do about that. The objective should always be to create a portfolio that is focused on growth because there is no way for you to always avoid losses. When things get tough, it is essential to keep calm and rationalize your decisions. Create an emergency investment plan and stick to it until the crisis passes. The best strategy in a crisis is to wait for it to be over. The more you panic, the greater the chance of making stupid investment decisions. That is why it is very important to stay prepared in all aspects of your financial journey so that you don't have to panic sell investments. Create a comprehensive financial and investment plan that will protect you in all circumstances. This will not happen in a day and will take a lot of time to devise and execute. Stay consistent and don't panic! You got this!

(P.S. Look for the bonus chapters right after this for additional tips on retirement planning and investment in REITs.)

# Conclusion

Dividends can play a major role in enhancing your investment portfolio. If you have been investing for some time, you know that market fluctuations can happen at any time. Even the best-performing stocks can quickly start making losses. Irrespective of the past performance of the stock, it can suddenly become loss-making due to adverse market conditions. There is absolutely no guarantee in the stock market, but does that mean you will not invest in it? Definitely not. Risks and uncertainties are integral parts of the investment journey, but you have to do your part to mitigate them and create a profitable portfolio for yourself.

Equity investments are inherently riskier because, unlike bonds, there are no fixed returns. However, dividends can change this perception. When you buy a dividend-paying stock, you are actually ensuring a certain rate of return on your investments. In the long run, this can help you tremendously, especially when there is a market downturn and the stocks are not performing well in terms of increase in value.

Moreover, dividend stocks are attractive to all investors which makes these stocks more expensive over time.

Once dividends are announced by a company, there is always a sharp positive movement in the stock prices because investors want to have a slice of the profits. When you hold these stocks for a long time, you will be able to reap a lot of profit from them. That is why it is very important to choose the right companies that will be able to provide you with these returns throughout your holding period. Dividends and their subsequent investing can become a deciding factor in your investment journey which is why you have to be aware of all the associated concepts.

There are various dividend models that we have discussed in this book that give you an insight into dividend growth and their discounting. This is the gateway to understanding dividend investing and subsequently portfolio management strategies. As your dividends grow over time, you should familiarize yourself with dividend growth investing and how you can choose the appropriate growth stocks. While making these selections, you must be aware of prioritizing your financial goals so that you can maximize the benefits of dividend growth investing. None of the portfolio management strategies will work if you are not sure about what you want and how you want to achieve them.

In Chapter 5, we have discussed several dividends investing strategies that will help you when you get started on this journey. These strategies are market-tested and have been effective for numerous investors all over the world. However, there is no universal strategy that will work for everyone and you must evaluate them according to your risk appetite and financial priorities. Understanding yourself and your goals is the most effective portfolio management tip that you can give yourself! You are different from the next person which is why their strategies might not be valid for you. Start small, so that even if you misstep, you do not end up making a huge loss.

The biggest secret of dividend investing is the compounding of dividends and reinvesting the same. You have to be active in your dividend investing process because the more you act on it, the better will be the effect of compounding to yield high results. Dividend investing can help you earn a lot of profits but you should be willing to explore different strategies. It is very important to include dividend investing in your portfolio and not treat it as something separate from your regular investment activities. Dividend investing should be a part of your investment portfolio that helps you grow your finances over time.

Throughout the chapters of this book, I have tried to include all the advanced details about dividend investing and portfolio management so that it helps you to understand dividends and work with them appropriately. Feel free to flip through whenever you are in doubt. Dividend investing can be complicated and confusing but if you keep at it and learn the mechanics of the process, you will become an expert at it in no time. The most important thing about any investing strategy is to be thorough and stay consistent in your efforts. If you can do that, you will be able to take on any crisis that the financial markets throw at you!

I hope my book was able to help you enhance your knowledge about dividends and dividend investing strategies. If you liked what you read, please let me know by leaving a review. Happy investing!

Chapter 8:

# Bonus Chapter 1: Retirement

Although everyone knows that they will have to stop working at some point in the future, retirement often comes as a surprise for many people. They are unable to visualize their life without a job and that is what creates a major problem. Things are very different when you don't have a job and if you do not plan, you will never be able to maintain your standard of living. That is why no discussion about investment planning can be complete without retirement planning. In this bonus chapter, we will walk you through the basics of retirement planning and what you need to do to prepare yourself financially for the next innings of your life.

# Factors to Consider for Retirement Planning

Planning for your retirement is a long process that you need to do over time. There are a lot of factors involved that you should consider ensuring you have everything for a comfortable retirement. Retirement planning will be different according to your age and your financial priorities but there are certain common factors for everyone.

## *Time Horizon*

If you are in your 20s or 30s, you have a lot of time to earn money and use it for creating a nest egg. This gives you the flexibility to invest in riskier instruments like stocks. If you consider the historical statistics, you will find that stocks have given higher returns in comparison to bonds or other fixed-income-bearing instruments. A person in their 30s should consider investing heavily in stocks because they will get the benefit of compounding. On the other hand, a person who is in their 40s or 50s should focus more on preserving their capital. This would entail investing heavily in bonds and other "safe" financial instruments so that they can earn a comfortable return and keep their principal amount intact.

## *Retirement Spending Needs*

Your standard of living now will determine how much you will be spending after your retirement. One of the biggest surprises after retirement is that people no longer have a steady income stream. However, they are unwilling to compromise their quality of life. This means that people end up spending more than what they are making which in turn results in financial distress. As a rational person, you should be very clear about your spending needs and other financial priorities so that you don't end up getting ugly surprises after retirement.

## *Assess Your Risk Tolerance*

The biggest mistake most people make is that they compare their retirement plans with others. Every person is unique and they have a distinct set of beliefs when it comes to investment decisions and retirement goals. That is why your risk tolerance and financial priorities will play an important part in your retirement plans. If you feel that you are not comfortable taking a huge amount of risk, then don't. The plan that you make should work for you in all stages.

## *Estate Planning*

Although it sounds like something only the "super rich" people do, estate planning is a very important part of your retirement planning process. Estate planning usually includes consulting with professionals like lawyers and accountants who can help you with asset allocation and creating wills. This will help you to ensure that you are making adequate plans for yourself and your next of kin after you retire. Investing in life insurance is an important part of estate planning which can again help you tremendously when you are no longer working.

# Steps to Retirement Planning

Retirement planning will look different for everyone depending on their income and other financial and non-financial priorities. Despite these differences, here are a few common steps that everyone can follow while they are planning for retirement.

1. **Decide Your Retirement Time:** You should be very clear about your retirement age because it will give you a perspective of how much money you need to save. For instance, if you wish to retire at 60 and currently you are 35 years old, then you have around 25 years to make all the necessary provisions. Having a clear goal in mind will help you to organize your

finances and plan accordingly. When you decide upon retirement age, you understand how much time you have left until you will no longer have a steady stream of regular income.

2. **Start Early:** Once you have decided upon retirement age, you can start saving up. The general rule is that the earlier you start, the better it will be for your finances. When you start early, you will also be able to avail the benefit of compounding which can give your savings a significant boost. People who are in their 20s or even 30s do not think about retirement because it seems like something that will not happen anytime soon. However, you should be prepared and get into the retirement planning mindset as soon as you can because it will give you the much-needed push to start setting aside money.

3. **Determine How Much You Need:** This can be tricky because it is difficult to ascertain the exact figure that will help you with a comfortable retirement. You can start with your current levels of income and the amount of money that you need to meet all your monthly expenses. Think about a figure and try to fixate on its achievability. Even if it seems like a lot right now, remember that you have many years to save up that money. For instance, if you think your retirement corpus is $1 million, then don't freak out. You don't have to make a million dollars today and it is perfectly achievable if you make a well-defined plan.

4. **Future Value of Current Savings:** Now let us do some math about retirement savings. To understand your finances and savings correctly, you have to determine the future value of your current savings. This is a mathematical way to ascertain how much your current savings will be worth after a specific period considering the time value of money. Depending on the prevalent inflation levels and other external factors, you can easily determine how much your present savings will turn out

to be after a certain period. You can use online calculators to get a reasonably correct estimate.

5. **Cut Back:** The most effective way to ensure all your retirement plans are being followed is to do a deep dive into all your expenses and cut back wherever you can. Remember that you are in this for the long haul and you need to be mindful of the areas in which you are spending your money.

6. **Manage Your Portfolio:** Depending on your age and risk appetite, balance your investment portfolio to ensure you are getting the most out of the money you are setting aside. Create a portfolio of stocks and bonds so that there is a proper risk-return trade-off.

## Investment Plans for Retirement

When you are planning to save money for retirement, you should have a distinct plan as to how and where you will be putting your money. Stocks are a good option when you are trying to invest money and earn a good return but you have to diversify your portfolio so that you can optimize the returns. Here are a few popular investment plans that are very suitable for retirement.

## *Defined Contribution Plans*

According to a recent study by insurance broker Willis Towers Watson, around 86% of Fortune 500 companies offered only defined contribution plans rather than traditional pensions in 2019 (Royal, 2022). This speaks volumes for the popularity of such plans in the context of creating a retirement corpus. These plans include a steady monthly contribution from the employee (which is often matched by the employer). Such contribution goes directly toward the retirement savings of the employee and they are usually not allowed to withdraw such funds before the expiry of a specific period.

## *IRAs*

IRA is a government-created plan to help people save up for their retirement. Here are the different types of IRAs that will help you understand which one is the most suitable for you:

- **Traditional IRA:** A traditional IRA is a popular retirement plan where you contribute from your pre-tax income. You get tax benefits for such contributions but the income from this plan is liable for taxes.

- **Roth IRA:** Contributions to a Roth IRA are done from after-tax income (Folger, 2022). This means that you will never have to pay taxes on any contributions or even withdrawals on retirement.

- **Spousal IRA:** A spousal IRA is a joint IRA plan, where your spouse can contribute to the plan too. The income of such a spouse must be greater than the amount of contribution being made to the IRA (Royal, 2022).

- **Rollover IRA:** If you wish to move your money from one retirement account (like a 401(k) account or another IRA), then you can use the rollover IRA to continue taking the tax advantages.

- **SEP IRA:** SEP IRA is exclusively for individuals and small businesses and their employees. SEP IRA contributions for every employee act as an alternative to a trust fund.

- **SIMPLE IRA:** In comparison to the 401(k) plans, SIMPLE IRAs are more convenient to employers because of the absence of nondiscrimination tests. Employers can provide a 3% match or contribute 2% even if the employee is not saving anything under this plan (Royal, 2022).

## *Traditional Pensions*

Pensions and cash balance plans are a part of defined benefit plans and are not widely used now. In these plans, the employer would be paying a fixed amount to the employee every month after they retire. Since it requires a lot of investment from the employer and the formalities are extremely heavy, they have lost their popularity and have been replaced by defined contribution plans.

## *401(k) Plans*

401(k) plans are defined contribution plans that are employer-sponsored and the employee gets a tax advantage when they contribute to such plans. You can choose to contribute a specified amount every month and it will keep growing until you withdraw the entire amount after you retire. To ensure that this plan is actually being used for retirement, there are tax implications and penalties when you withdraw money from this fund before retirement age.

## *Cash Value Insurance Plan*

Many employers provide insurance as a retirement plan. These insurance vehicles usually protect the employee after their retirement and can be in the form of a lump sum payment after retirement or after the death of the employee.

## *Investment in Long-Term Stocks*

Long-term stocks can be a game-changer in your retirement portfolio. Investing in stocks of bluechip companies and holding them for long periods have fetched the investors huge amounts of return. Usually, these stocks are not suitable for trading because the prices don't change very frequently. However, in the long haul, these stocks show significant appreciation which in turn leads to capital growth for the investor.

## *Dividend Investing*

If you are holding dividend-paying stocks, you will receive dividends in periodic frequencies. Investing such dividends into various channels or using the dividend to buy more stocks can be a great way to build up your retirement corpus.

Real estate investments are great options when you are planning for your retirement. Apart from all the other investment options mentioned in this chapter, real estate can also be a very useful tool in your retirement journey. In the next bonus chapter, we will focus on Real Estate Investment Trusts (REITs) and why they are a great option to include in your retirement plans.

Chapter 9:

# Bonus Chapter 2: REITs

Real estate has always been considered to be one of the most lucrative forms of investment. This is because historically it has always increased in value and provided great returns to its holders. However, despite being an attractive investment choice, it has stayed inaccessible to many investors because of the high initial investment. Property has always been an expensive asset and you needed a lot of money to buy it. Over time, developments in the credit and financing sector have made it easier for many people to buy property both for residential and investment purposes. Nowadays, with the introduction of Real Estate Investment Trusts (REITs), investors can get a slice of the real estate profits without putting in too much money (Folger, 2019). In this chapter, we will talk about what REITs are and how they can become a great addition to your investment portfolio.

# Understanding REITs

So this brings us to the most obvious question: what exactly are REITs? A REIT is a company that is involved solely in owning, operating, and financing income-generating real estate (Chen, 2022). Structurally, REITs follow the design of mutual funds and have a large pool of investors, who receive dividends from real estate without the hassle of owning or managing any property.

## *How do REITs Work?*

REITs were established in 1960, as an amendment to the Cigar Excise Tax Extension and allowed people to own shares in commercial real estate portfolios (Chen, 2022). Before REITs, such ownership was exclusively limited to wealthy investors, and it could be done through large financial intermediaries. The introduction of REITs played an important role in opening up the real estate sector to regular individual investors. They could now own real estate shares without owning the physical property and in turn, earn profits from this sector.

The workings of a REIT are similar to that of a mutual fund. A REIT can have several properties in its portfolio including but not limited to apartment complexes, data centers, healthcare facilities, hotels, infrastructure, office buildings, retail centers, self-storage, timberland, and warehouses (Chen, 2022). Usually, REITs specialize in a specific sector but there can be diversified REITs that earn their revenues from a variety of real estate investments. The REIT would either finance or manage these properties under their portfolio and then distribute the income earned from them to the investors who have funded the REIT. This is an efficient process that helps investors from all affordability levels to invest in real estate.

## *Types of REITs*

Usually, REITs can be classified into the following three types:

- **Equity REIT:** Equity REITs are the most common types of REITs in the market, and they are primarily involved in the owning and managing of real estate (Nickolas, 2019). The primary source of income for Equity REITs is rent from the properties that they hold in their portfolio.

- **Mortgage REIT:** Mortgage REITs pertain to property financing and they provide loans to real estate owners or acquire mortgage-backed securities. Mortgage REITs procure funding from investors at a certain rate of interest and provide loans to property buyers at a higher rate. The primary source of income for mortgage REITs is this net income margin. Although Mortgage REITs are very profitable, they are sensitive to variations in interest rates (Chen, 2022).

- **Hybrid REIT:** Hybrid REITs can earn their income from both owning real estate and financing properties.

Apart from these types, there is another way in which REITs are classified. Based on how the shares of a REIT are traded, they can be classified into the following categories:

- **Publicly Traded REITs:** Publicly traded REITs can be bought, sold, and traded on stock markets like regular stocks and are regulated by U.S. Securities and Exchange Commission (Chen, 2022). These REITs have a high level of liquidity since they can be easily bought and sold.

- **Public Non-traded REITs:** Also regulated by the SEC, these REITs cannot be traded like publicly traded REITs even though they are public and that is why they are less liquid (Corporate Finance Institute, 2022). However, due to their exclusivity, they are less vulnerable to market fluctuations and can offer good returns to their holders.

- **Private REITs:** Private REITs are privately regulated and are not available to regular investors. They are exclusive and can only be accessible by institutional investors in large volumes.

## *What Can Qualify as a REIT?*

Since REITs are still relatively new financial instruments, there are certain strict rules and regulations that they have to adhere to if they wish to be classified as REITs. The Internal Revenue Code (IRC) has laid down the following provisions for trusts and companies that are in the business of owning or financing real estate and then distributing profits to its shareholders.

- At least 75% of total assets should comprise real estate, cash, or US Treasuries (Chen, 2022b).

- At least 75% of the gross income should be earned from rent, interest on real estate mortgages, or other property sales.

- At least 90% of the income must be distributed to the shareholders.

- Must have a minimum of 100 shareholders after it has been operating for a year.

- Ownership cannot be condensed which means less than five shareholders cannot own more than 50% shares.

- The entity should be taxed as a corporation and managed by trustees or a board of directors.

# Pros and Cons of Investing in REITs

REITs are complex financial instruments that have some unique benefits and challenges. To become a successful REIT investor, you must understand how they work and what problems you might face. On that note, you should be aware of the pros and cons of REITs so that you can make well-informed decisions about them.

## *Pros*

- The biggest advantage of having REITs in your investment portfolio is that you get to enjoy the profits of the real estate sector without the hassles of owning and managing property.

- Publicly traded REITs can be easily bought and sold on the stock markets which gives them a high level of liquidity like regular stocks. Investors can trade REITs without any problems, and they can enjoy the associated profits promptly.

- REITs can offer a wide range of diversification benefits even within the real estate sector. For example, if you invest in hybrid REITs, you can expose yourself to the income from owning properties and financing real estate mortgages.

- Since REITs are governed by the IRC, there is a high level of transparency in these securities.

- Historically, real estate has been considered a stable investment which subsequently makes REITs extremely stable and reliable financial instruments. Just like actual real estate, REITs can act as a hedge against inflation and provide competitive risk-adjusted returns (Chen, 2022).

## *Cons*

- Despite high claims of liquidity, public non-traded REITs and private REITs are highly illiquid. The buying and selling of these REITs occur through private modes and are often limited to institutional investors.

- Since REITs are still new, there are often risks of fraud associated with them. Investors are not aware of the formalities that REITs have to adhere to which is why they end up investing in fraudulent schemes that pose to be REITs.

- REITs are susceptible to market risk which means the returns are not always as high as they are portrayed to be. The growth rate is comparatively lower and there is no guarantee that there will be any returns.

# REIT Fraud

REITs are complex and despite their popularity, most investors are yet to understand how they work. Because of the inherent ignorance associated with REITs, many people have become victims of REIT fraud and other similar scams. As a rational investor, you must be aware of such issues and make sure that you are only investing in legitimate REITs. The registration of both publicly traded and publicly non-traded REITs can be verified through the SEC's EDGAR system (Chen, 2022). Investors are encouraged to check the same before they invest in them. If you are not sure about the legitimacy, you should not invest in private REITs. If a REIT was recommended to you by a specific broker or financial intermediary, make sure to check their records using the free tool provided by SEC. There are various resources available online that you must check out before you invest in REITs to protect yourself from any scam.

REITs can be a great addition to your investment portfolio because of the stability that it brings. Real estate has always been considered a hedge against inflation which means that even during severe economic downturns, real estate investments perform well. Following that principle, REITs can also be considered a good investment. However, you should be vigilant about REIT frauds because it is still a relatively new financial instrument that is yet to get completely developed. Do your research before you invest to ensure that you are not putting your money in a fraudulent scheme.

# Glossary

**401 (k) Plan:** 401(k) plans are defined contribution plans that are employer-sponsored, and the employee gets a tax advantage when they contribute to such plans. You can choose to contribute a specified amount every month and it will keep growing until you withdraw the entire amount after you retire. To ensure that this plan is actually being used for retirement, there are tax implications and penalties when you withdraw money from this fund before retirement age.

**Active Portfolio Management:** In active portfolio management, the manager deals with closed-end funds and tries to beat the performance of the index by actively buying and selling investments (Hayes, 2019a). In such cases, the portfolio is dynamic, and managers use different kinds of analytical techniques to ensure that the stocks they are choosing will yield the maximum results.

**Arithmetic Mean:** Arithmetic mean is a statistical term that denotes the simple average of a list of values. For example, consider the following set of values: 20, 25, 30, 35, 40. The arithmetic mean of these values will be calculated as $(20+25+30+35+40)/5 = 30$

**Asset Allocation:** Asset allocation is the process of allotting money to specific securities based on the financial priorities and risk appetite of the investors. This would include choosing stocks and other financial instruments that are both volatile and non-volatile so that the investor can expose themselves to a variety of market elements and earn profits in the process.

**Bear Market Investing Strategies:** It is very important to have a distinct set of bear market investing strategies because we are living in times of severe economic uncertainties. Bear markets are characterized by reductions in prices, and everyone is freaked out because they have no idea how they will handle such difficult times. Bear market investing strategies will ensure that you have enough financial backup to support yourself through adversities. These strategies can include dollar cost averaging, playing dead, diversification, and including cash in the portfolio.

**Bear Market:** A bear market is a period when the whole financial markets experience severe and prolonged fall in prices. It is a condition when the overall prices of securities fall more than 20% from the recent highs and there is a widespread negative attitude in the market that dampens investor spirits (Chen, 2019). Bear markets are fairly common, and they occur frequently which is why you have to prepare yourself and your portfolio to withstand the same. The recent COVID-19 pandemic brought about severe economic downturns and ushered in another bear market period.

**Beta:** A bear market is a period when the whole financial markets experience severe and prolonged fall in prices. It is a condition when the overall prices of securities fall more than 20% from the recent highs and there is a widespread negative attitude in the market that dampens investor spirits (Chen, 2019). Bear markets are fairly common, and they occur frequently which is why you have to prepare yourself and your portfolio to withstand the same. The recent COVID-19 pandemic brought about severe economic downturns and ushered in another bear market period.

**Capital Asset Pricing Model:** The Capital Asset Pricing Model is a financial model that attempts to establish a relationship between expected returns, risk-free market returns, and beta to find out the cost of equity of a particular stock (Kenton, 2022).

**Cash Dividend:** Cash dividends are paid to the shareholders in the form of cash.

**Cash Value Insurance Plan:** Many employers provide insurance as a retirement plan. These insurance vehicles usually protect the employee after their retirement and can be in the form of a lump sum payment after retirement or after the expiry of the employee.

**Compounding:** Compounding is the process where a person earns interest on the principal along with interest.

**Constitution of REITs:** Internal Revenue Code (IRC) has laid down the following provisions for trusts and companies that are in the business of owning or financing real estate and then distributing profits to its shareholders: 75% of total assets should comprise real estate, cash, or US Treasuries, 75% of the gross income should be earned from rent, interest on real estate mortgages, or other property sales, 90% of the income must be distributed to the shareholders, must have a minimum of 100 shareholders after it has been operating for a year, five or lesser shareholders cannot hold more than 50% of the shares, and the entity should be taxed as a corporation and managed by trustees or a board of directors.

**Cost Base of DRIPs:** Most companies offer DRIPs to their investors to convert the dividend that they have earned into more shares of the same stock. As mentioned before, it is a great way to increase your earnings and grow your capital over time. However, it is important to keep a track of the cost base that is used by DRIPs to make sure the price at which the new stocks are being acquired. The cost base is the price that the DRIPs are considering for acquiring the additional units with the dividend that has been earned by the investor. Since the prices are continuously fluctuating, it is important to ensure that you are not losing any value in procuring new units.

**Cutting Back:** Cutting back means reducing the number of routine expenses that you have. The most effective way to ensure all your retirement plans are being followed is to do a deep dive into all your expenses and cut back wherever you can. Remember that you are in this for the long haul, and you need to be mindful of the areas in which you are spending your money.

**Defined Contribution Plans:** Defined plans include a steady monthly contribution from the employee (which is often matched by the employer). Such contribution goes directly toward the retirement savings of the employee, and they are usually not allowed to withdraw such funds before the expiry of a specific period. According to a recent study by insurance broker Willis Towers Watson, around 86% of Fortune 500 companies offered only defined contribution plans rather than traditional pensions in 2019 (Royal, 2022).

**Discounting:** According to financial expert James Chen (2019), "Discounting is the process of determining the present value of a payment or a stream of payments that is to be received in the future. Given the time value of money, a dollar is worth more today than it would be worth tomorrow. Discounting is the primary factor used in pricing a stream of tomorrow's cash flows."

**Diversification:** Diversification is the process of allocating money to different kinds of assets that would create a well-balanced portfolio. This helps the investor in earning profits while mitigating the risks related to stock market investments. It is an essential part of the portfolio management process and involves choosing securities from different industries and volatility levels.

**Dividend Component of Returns:** Most new investors tend to discard the impact of dividends as a part of their total returns. However, as a dividend growth investor, you must understand the role that dividends play in the total returns earned from a stock. According to a study on the impact of dividends on S & P 500 Funds published by Hartford funds, it was found that from December 1960 through December 2018, 82% of the index's total return consisted of dividends that were reinvested along with its compounding value that accrued during this period (Farrington, 2019).

**Dividend Discount Model:** The dividend discount model (DDM) is an analytical financial analysis model that calculates the present value of a company's stock price by adding the discounted value of all the future dividends that it will pay over a specified period (Chen, 2022a). This model is one of the most accurate dividend valuation models because it considers the time value of money and other prevailing market conditions like returns and payout factors to calculate the fair value of a stock. After calculation through the DDM method is done, the fair value of the stock is compared with the current price. If the fair value is greater than the price, then the stock is undervalued and if the fair value is lesser then the stock is overvalued. Investors and analysts frequently use these comparisons to make purchase decisions and try to figure out which market position would be the most profitable.

**Dividend Growth Investing:** Dividend growth investing targets the growth elements in the dividends that you are earning. Since the size of the markets is continuously increasing, it is a general assumption that returns will increase over time. Dividend growth investors try to capture this growth and use it to increase the value of their portfolio. The most common way to do this is by reinvesting the cash received to buy additional units of the same stock or other high-paying stocks. Investors can use DRIPs to easily convert their cash into shares of the same stock. Many investors like to spice it up and use the cash for other high-return stocks as well. This enables them to buy newer stocks without paying any money. Dividend growth investing can be a very lucrative scheme for investors if they choose the right stocks.

**Dividend Growth Model:** The dividend growth model is a financial model that helps in the calculation of the fair value of the stock. To do so, it uses the value of dividends that have been distributed by the stock in the past. It is assumed that the dividends either grow at a constant rate forever till perpetuity or at a varying rate for a given period. This model tries to establish a relationship between the fair value of a company's stock price, the current dividend of the company, and the rate at which it will grow in the future (Price, 2022). It is expressed as the following mathematical formula:

*Price = Current annual dividend ÷ (Desired rate of return-Expected rate of dividend growth)* (Chen, 2020)

**Dividend Growth Rate:** According to financial expert James Chen (2020), "The dividend growth rate is the annualized percentage rate of growth that a particular stock's dividend undergoes over a period of time. Many mature companies seek to increase the dividends paid to their investors on a regular basis. Knowing the dividend growth rate is a key input for stock valuation models known as dividend discount models." Dividend growth is an integral part of the dividend discounting model and can be calculated using the arithmetic mean or a compound growth rate. Calculating the dividend growth rate is essential to understand how much dividend income a stock is capable of generating.

**Dividend Growth:** Dividend growth is the concept where we use a growth rate to understand how the dividends have been increasing or decreasing over time. Most companies that have a proven track record of paying regular dividends have an increasing dividend growth rate.

This is a great metric for dividend investors because dividend growth is what they must be aiming for in the long run. A company that shows consistent dividend growth has got great financial health and a solid cash flow because it is continuously dividing its profits among its shareholders. Most investors consider dividend growth to be suitable for people seeking passive income from their investments. However, dividend growth can be helpful for all categories of investors because the growth will ultimately help them in growing their portfolios.

**Dividend Investing:** Dividend investing is the process of buying dividend-paying stocks and then investing the dividends received from them to buy additional units of the same stock or increase the value of your portfolio by making other investments. Apart from providing a steady income stream, dividend investing helps in enhancing your portfolio and contributes to growth (Kennon, 2022).

**Dividend Payout Ratio:** This is a ratio between the dividend paid by the company and the net earnings earned by it in a certain accounting period. A very high dividend payout ratio is a good indication that there will not be any problems even if there is a downward market fluctuation. On the other hand, if the dividend payout ratio is very low and moves around zero, then you should think twice before buying the stock because it might not be dividend-paying. The dividend payout ratio varies between accounting periods because the figure of net income is usually taken from the financial statements prepared by the company.

**Dividend Reinvestment Programs (DRIPs):** Dividend Reinvestment Programs (DRIPs) are special schemes created by companies where shareholders can reinvest shares that they have received as a dividend. Such reinvestment will be done at a discount, which means that the shareholder will be able to procure more shares at a lesser price. DRIPs are not mandatory for the shareholder, and they usually have the choice of accepting the dividends in cash.

**Dividend Yield Ratio:** This is one of the most common metrics of dividend investing and is calculated as the ratio between dividends and stock price. Although this is a fundamental metric, it cannot be used in isolation, and it works well when you combine it with other dividend investing ratios. The dividend yield is also not the most stable metric because it can suddenly increase or decrease with dramatic fluctuations in the share price. If there is a decrease in stock price due to an internal conflict in the company, then the dividend yield will be higher even though it is not a representation of higher dividend payouts (Mohan, 2021).

**Dividend Yield:** We have already talked about the calculation of the dividend yield ratio. The concept of dividend yield refers to the number of dividend earnings that a stock is providing in a given period. Usually, it is represented in an annualized format which is calculated by multiplying the quarterly dividend rates by four. For example, if the dividend per share (annualized) is $5 and the price of the share is $80, then the dividend yield is 5/80 or 6.25%. The dividend yield is usually expressed as a percentage of the stock price. Although it is widely used by investors, the dividend yield is not always a great indicator of how the stock is doing. In fact, it does not even provide a proper representation of the dividends that are being distributed.

**Dividend:** Dividends are the distribution of a company's earnings to its shareholders either in the form of cash or reinvestment in more stocks of the company (Hayes, 2022). Usually, dividends are paid on a quarterly basis (although this is not a fixed rule) and if you own the shares before the date of dividend declaration, you will be eligible for the same.

**Dollar Cost Averaging:** Dollar-cost averaging is an investment strategy that helps people to deal with uncertain economic times by automating investment amounts (Chen, 2021). In this method, you will be investing a specific amount every month (or at any specific periodic intervals) and this will help in reducing the average cost of the investments over time, which in turn helps in lowering the effect of price volatility on your portfolio.

**Equity REIT:** Equity REITs are primarily involved in the owning and managing of real estate and are the most common. The primary source of income for Equity REITs is rent from the properties that they hold in their portfolio.

**Equity Valuation:** Equity valuation is a comprehensive technique used by analysts to find out the value of a company's equity. Some of the common tools used in equity valuation include fundamental analysis and technical analysis.

**Estate Planning:** The process of making arrangements and specifying who will be entitled to what part of your estate in your absence. This process usually includes consulting with professionals like lawyers and accountants who can help you with asset allocation and creating wills.

**Franking Credits:** Countries like Australia have dividend imputation tax credits which are also known as franking credits (Mohan, 2021). With the help of these franking credits, an individual investor can claim a tax credit on their dividend income because the company has already paid taxes on their profits. This is a very effective way for the individual taxpayer to save money on taxes in the event the tax rate is very high on the earned dividends. Many times, the taxes paid by the company is more than the tax rate of the individual and in such cases, they will receive refunds from the tax authorities.

**Fundamental Analysis:** In terms of a company's valuation, fundamental analysis refers to the process of analyzing the overall economic and financial factors to understand the intrinsic value of a stock (Segal, 2019). The main objective of fundamental analysis is to understand whether a security is over or under-valued. Fundamental analysis mostly uses business results related to earnings and other financials.

**Future Value of Current Savings:** This is a mathematical way to ascertain how much your current savings will be worth after a specific period considering the time value of money.

**Gordon Growth Model:** The Gordon Growth Model is a financial model that helps in the calculation of the fair value of the stock. To do so, it uses the value of dividends that have been distributed by the stock in the past. It is calculated with the help of the following formula:

*P = D1 ÷ (r - g), where*

*P = Currency price of the stock*

*D1 = Last paid dividend*

*r=* *Required rate of return*

*g=* *Constant growth rate that will continue till perpetuity*

**Growth Indicator of Healthy Operations:** As a rational investor, you should always consider growth as the more important determinant than yield. A company that is paying a high dividend per share today might not always be able to sustain itself in the long run. There have been numerous instances where companies that pay large dividends have failed to keep up their yield and then faced natural decline. While high yield is an attractive quality in a dividend stock, growth is the indicator of stability. If you look at it from a comprehensive viewpoint, growth shows that the operating environment of a company is healthy.

**Hybrid REIT:** Hybrid REITs earn their income from both owning real estate and financing properties.

**Inflation:** Inflation is the economic phenomenon where prices of goods and services keep on increasing over time.

**IRA:** IRA is an acronym for Individual Retirement Account. It is a government-created plan to help people save up for their retirement. There are various types of IRAs including traditional IRA, simple IRA, Roth IRA, rollover IRA, spousal IRA, and others.

**Long:** In investing, long or going long means buying more units of the investment or simply buying.

**Monthly Dividend Income:** As a dividend investor, you need to track your income from your dividends regularly to determine how much you are earning and how your dividends are growing. The best way to do this is by tracking your monthly income from your dividends. You can use any online tool to filter out your monthly income or simply calculate the total dividend income received from a stock in a year and then divide the figure by 12. For example, if you have received $150 per quarter as dividends from a stock, then your annual income would be $600 and your monthly income would be $600/12= $50.

**Mortgage REIT:** Mortgage REITs pertain to property financing and they provide loans to real estate owners or acquire mortgage-backed securities. Mortgage REITs procure funding from investors at a certain rate of interest and provide loans to property buyers at a higher rate. The primary source of income for mortgage REITs is this net income margin. Although Mortgage REITs are very profitable, they are sensitive to variations in interest rates (Chen, 2022).

**Negative Beta:** A negative beta would indicate that there is an inverse relationship between the stock and the index. This does not happen because stocks and the index tend to have the same trends. Real estate and gold might have negative beta because they perform well even when the market is falling but there is no conclusive evidence to establish the same. However, if you find any security that has a negative beta, you should consider investing in it because it will act as a hedge against market risk.

**Ordinary Dividend:** An ordinary dividend is one where the shareholder has held the stocks for less than 61 days in the period of 121 days that started one business day before the date of declaration of the dividend (Reiff, 2022).

**Paperwork for Dividend Investing:** There is a lot of paperwork associated with the dividend investing process. If you are holding dividend-paying stocks of multiple companies, then you have to keep track of when the dividends are being announced, what is the present rate, and other necessary details to ensure that the dividend investing process is being executed properly.

**Passive Portfolio Management:** Passive portfolio management is synonymous with investing in index funds which is why it is also known as indexing or index investing (Hayes, 2019a). It is a suitable strategy for passive investors who wish to invest money for the long term and do not want to keep switching investments. The general notion is that index funds will grow over time which makes this strategy quite useful for investors with a long time horizon.

**Play Dead:** The term "playing dead" stems from the fact that if you encounter a bear in a forest, the best strategy would be to act as if you are dead to ensure that the bear does not attack you. Here, the wild bear is a metaphor for the bear markets, and when there are widespread price reductions, staying calm and playing dead is a great strategy. As a part of this policy, you can choose to shift funds from the stock market to safer securities certificates of deposit (CDs), U.S. Treasury bills, and other highly liquid instruments that have shorter maturity periods (Investopedia, 2022).

**Portfolio Management:** Portfolio management can be regarded as the art and science of choosing investments according to the specific needs of an individual or institution that will help them to maximize their earnings in their specified time horizon (Hayes, 2019a). It is an important process that helps investor to achieve their investment objectives and handle all kinds of market risk.

**Preferred Dividends:** These are dividends that are paid to holders of preferred stocks.

**Preferred Stocks:** Preferred stocks have the functions of both a stock and a bond. They usually provide a fixed rate of return to their holders like a bond but have the risky nature of a stock. Preferred stocks usually yield more returns than bonds.

**Private REITs:** Private REITs are privately regulated and are not available to regular investors. They are exclusive and can only be accessible by institutional investors in large volumes.

**Public Non-Traded REITs:** Also regulated by the SEC, these REITs cannot be traded like publicly traded REITs even though they are public and that is why they are less liquid (Corporate Finance Insitute, 2022). However, due to their exclusivity, they are less vulnerable to market fluctuations and can offer good returns to their holders.

**Publicly Traded REITs:** Publicly traded REITs can be bought, sold, and traded on stock markets like regular stocks and are regulated by U.S. Securities and Exchange Commission (Chen, 2022). These REITs have a high level of liquidity since they can be easily bought and sold.

**Qualified Dividend:** A qualified dividend is one where the shareholder has held the stocks for more than 61 days in the period of 121 days that started one business day before the date of declaration of the dividend (Reiff, 2022). A qualified dividend is eligible for lower rates of capital gain tax.

**Real Estate Investment Trust (REIT):** A REIT is a company that is involved solely in owning, operating, and financing income-generating real estate (Chen, 2022). Structurally, REITs follow the design of mutual funds and have a large pool of investors who earn dividends from real estate without the hassle of property ownership or management.

**Rebalancing:** The process of portfolio management is not static and needs to change along with changing market conditions. That is why portfolio rebalancing is an important part because it involves changing the asset allocations to ensure that the investor is getting a higher yield from their investments. Rebalancing helps to keep the portfolio relevant according to the requirements and market trends.

**REIT Fraud:** Because of the inherent ignorance associated with REITs, many people have become victims of REIT fraud and other similar scams. As a rational investor, you must be aware of such issues and make sure that you are only investing in legitimate REITs. The registration of both publicly traded and publicly non-traded REITs can be verified through the SEC's EDGAR system (Chen, 2022).

**Retirement Spending Needs:** Retirement spending needs are determined by your standard of living now. One of the biggest surprises after retirement is that people no longer have a steady income stream. However, they are unwilling to compromise their quality of life. This means that people end up spending more than what they are making which in turn results in financial distress. As a rational person, you should be very clear about your spending needs and other financial priorities so that you don't end up getting ugly surprises after retirement.

**Risk-Adjusted Return:** Risk-adjusted return is the process of calculating the return on a potential investment by considering the degree of risk that the investor needs to undertake for earning such a return. It is one of the most accurate ways to evaluate the profitability of an investment and whether it will be feasible to put money into it.

**Risk-Free Return:** The risk-free return is the rate of return that is earned by safe government securities like treasury bills.

**Risk Appetite:** Risk appetite is considered to be the amount of risk an organization or individual is ready to undertake to achieve its objectives (Shackleford, 2021).

**Risk Averse:** In terms of investment decisions, a risk-averse person is someone who does not like risk elements in their investment portfolio. Usually, these people would prefer to invest in bonds and other fixed-income-bearing securities.

**Risk Lover:** In terms of investment decisions, a risk lover is a person who likes to undertake risk as a part of their investment decisions. These people would like to invest in stocks and other high-risk investment vehicles.

**Risk Neutral:** In terms of investment decisions, a risk-neutral person is not concerned with the element of risk elements in their investment portfolio.

**Risk Tolerance:** Risk tolerance is valid for individual investors. A person might have a high-risk appetite but that does not always mean they will have a high-risk tolerance level. Even if their circumstances demand them to undertake more risk, they might not have the stomach to actually go through with it. Risk tolerance is a sensitive concept and depends on a lot of factors like the financial condition of the person in the present situation.

**Rollover IRA:** If you wish to move your money from one retirement account (like a 401(k) account or another IRA), then you can use the rollover IRA to continue taking the tax advantages.

**Roth IRA:** Roth IRA contributions are done from after-tax income. This means that you will never have to pay taxes on any contributions or even withdrawals on retirement.

**S & P 500 Index Fund:** This is a fund that invests in the S & P 500 companies (Investopedia, 2020).

**S & P 500 Index:** The S & P 500 Index or the Standard & Poor's 500 Index is an index of the stock prices of the most powerful American companies (Investopedia, 2020).

**SEP IRA:** SEP IRA is exclusively for individuals and small businesses and their employees. Instead of putting the money in a trust fund, contributions in a SEP IRA are done for each employee.

**Short:** In investing, short or going short means to sell the existing holdings.

**SIMPLE IRA:** In comparison to the 401(k) plans, SIMPLE IRAs are more convenient to employers because of the absence of nondiscrimination tests. Employers can provide a 3% match or contribute 2% even if the employee is not saving anything under this plan (Royal, 2022).

**Special Dividends:** Special dividends are paid out of special or extraordinary earnings that the company does not need to accumulate any more. The company might have earned such income a long time ago and they want to put it to good use by distributing a special dividend on all classes of stocks. Unlike normal dividends, special dividends are not distributed at regular frequencies.

**Spousal IRA:** A spousal IRA is a joint IRA plan, where your spouse can contribute to the plan too. The income of such a spouse must be greater than the amount of contribution being made to the IRA (Royal, 2022).

**Stock Dividend:** Companies often decide to pay dividends in the form of additional stocks to the existing shareholders. These dividends are known as stock dividends.

**Stock:** Usually, the capital of a company is divided into several shares that are represented by stocks. Buying a stock means that the holder can become part owner of the company. For a publicly traded company, these stocks can be purchased by regular investors. A shareholder's ownership of a company is limited to the value of the stock that they hold.

**Systematic Risk:** Systematic risk is the risk that affects all the companies of a particular industry or all stocks in an index and is highly general in nature. It is also known as "undiversifiable risk," "volatility" or "market risk" (Chen, 2021a).

**Technical Analysis:** Technical analysis is the process of evaluating a company's stock prices with the help of statistical trends that have been gathered over the trading history and mainly concerns price movement and volume (Hayes, 2019). This type of analysis is heavily focused on price and volume and often uses complex statistical patterns to represent movements.

**Total Annualized Return:** Total annualized return is not exclusively related to dividend investing. However, it provides an exhaustive insight into the dividend investing process and helps investors to understand how much they are earning from their investments. Usually, total annualized return consists of elements like capital gains, dividends, currency fluctuations, brokerage, and time value of money (Mohan, 2021). It is used widely by all portfolio managers and investors to understand the health of their investments and the overall performance of their portfolios. Total annualized return is calculated as a ratio between the amount of return received and the amount invested and is influenced by all the elements mentioned above.

**Traditional IRA:** A traditional IRA is a popular retirement plan where you contribute from your pre-tax income. You get tax benefits for such contributions but the income from this plan is liable for taxes.

**Traditional Pensions:** Pensions are a part of defined benefit plans and are not widely used now. In these plans, the employer would be paying a fixed amount to the employee every month after they retire. Since it requires a lot of investment from the employer and the formalities are extremely heavy, they have lost their popularity and have been replaced by defined contribution plans. Cash balance plans are also examples of defined benefit plans.

**Unsystematic Risk:** Also known as non-systematic risk, specific risk, diversifiable risk, or residual risk, this type of risk is company-specific and can only be reduced with the help of portfolio diversification (Chen, 2021a).

**Zero Beta:** A security with zero beta means that it has no correlation with the market. This means that even if the market moves drastically, the value of the security will remain unchanged. Cash has a beta of zero because its value stays constant in all market conditions, provided there is no inflation (Investopedia, 2019).

# References

*7 investing strategies to prepare for bear markets.* (2022, May 20). Schwab Brokerage. https://www.schwab.com/learn/story/7-investing-strategies-to-prepare-bear-markets

Bloomenthal, A. (2022a, January 29). *How to pick the best dividend stocks.* Investopedia. https://www.investopedia.com/articles/active-trading/042315/top-dividend-stocks-how-pick-them.asp

Bloomenthal, A. (2022b, October 5). *How to invest in the S&P 500.* Investopedia. https://www.investopedia.com/ask/answers/how-can-i-buy-sp-500-fund/#:~:text=An%20S%26P%20500%20Index%20Fund%20is%20an%20investment%20composed%20of

Chen, J. (2019a). *Bear market definition.* Investopedia. https://www.investopedia.com/terms/b/bearmarket.asp

Chen, J. (2019b). *Discounting.* Investopedia. https://www.investopedia.com/terms/d/discounting.asp

Chen, J. (2020). *Learn about dividend growth rate.* Investopedia. https://www.investopedia.com/terms/d/dividendgrowthrate.asp

Chen, J. (2021a, April 8). *Unsystematic risk.* Investopedia. https://www.investopedia.com/terms/u/unsystematicrisk.asp#:~:text=management%2C%20and%20analytics.-

Chen, J. (2021b, April 29). *Systematic risk.* Investopedia. https://www.investopedia.com/terms/s/systematicrisk.asp

Chen, J. (2021c, August 19). *Dollar-Cost Averaging (DCA) definition*. Investopedia. https://www.investopedia.com/terms/d/dollarcostaveraging.asp

Chen, J. (2022a, March 6). *Dividend discount model – DDM*. Investopedia. https://www.investopedia.com/terms/d/ddm.asp

Chen, J. (2022b, April 4). *Real estate investment trust (REIT)*. Investopedia. https://www.investopedia.com/terms/r/reit.asp#toc-pros-and-cons-of-investing-in-reits

Corporate Finance Insitute. (2022, October 12). *Non-Traded REIT*. Corporate Finance Institute. https://corporatefinanceinstitute.com/resources/commercial-real-estate/non-traded-reit/

Corporate Finance Institute. (2022, June 16). *SMART goals*. Corporate Finance Institute; Corporate Finance Institute. https://corporatefinanceinstitute.com/resources/management/smart-goal/

Farrington, R. (2019, October 7). *What Is dividend growth investing and how to get started*. The College Investor. https://thecollegeinvestor.com/32466/dividend-growth-investing/

Folger, J. (2019). *Direct real estate investing versus REITs*. Investopedia. https://www.investopedia.com/articles/investing/072314/investing-real-estate-versus-reits.asp

Folger, J. (2022, October 28). *How Roth IRA taxes work*. Investopedia. https://www.investopedia.com/how-roth-ira-taxes-work-4769988

Groww. (2016). *What is portfolio management? Definition, types & objectives*. Groww; Groww. https://groww.in/p/portfolio-management

Hayes, A. (2019a). *Portfolio management definition*. Investopedia. https://www.investopedia.com/terms/p/portfoliomanagement.asp

Hayes, A. (2019b). *Technical analysis*. Investopedia. https://www.investopedia.com/terms/t/technicalanalysis.asp

Hayes, A. (2019c). *Understanding Gordon growth model*. Investopedia. https://www.investopedia.com/terms/g/gordongrowthmodel.asp

Hayes, A. (2022, June 28). *Dividends: Definition in stocks and how payments work*. Investopedia. https://www.investopedia.com/terms/d/dividend.asp#toc-dividend-paying-companies

Investopedia. (2019). *Using beta to understand a stock's risk*. Investopedia. https://www.investopedia.com/investing/beta-gauging-price-fluctuations/

Investopedia. (2020). *What does the S&P 500 Index measure and how is it calculated?* Investopedia. https://www.investopedia.com/ask/answers/040215/what-does-sp-500-index-measure-and-how-it-calculated.asp

Investopedia. (2022, May 30). *Ways to survive a market downturn*. Investopedia. https://www.investopedia.com/8-ways-to-survive-a-market-downturn-4773417#toc-accumulate-with-dollar-cost-averaging

Investor.gov. (n.d.). *Real Estate Investment Trusts (REITs) | Investor.gov*. Www.investor.gov. https://www.investor.gov/introduction-investing/investing-basics/investment-products/real-estate-investment-trusts-reits

Kagan, J. (2022, September 9). *5 key retirement planning steps that everyone should take*. Investopedia.

https://www.investopedia.com/articles/retirement/11/5-steps-to-retirement-plan.asp#toc-5-stay-on-top-of-estate-planning

Kennon, J. (2021, November 20). *Dividend growth investing: A long term solution.* The Balance. https://www.thebalancemoney.com/making-money-with-the-dividend-growth-investing-strategy-357877#toc-sub-strategies-for-dividend-growth-investing

Kennon, J. (2022, November 28). *Dividend investing.* The Balance. https://www.thebalancemoney.com/what-is-dividend-investing-357437#toc-strategies-for-dividend-investing

Kenton, W. (2022, October 24). *Capital Asset Pricing Model - CAPM.* Investopedia. https://www.investopedia.com/terms/c/capm.asp

Manoukian, J.-G. (2016, September 29). *Risk appetite and risk tolerance: What's the difference?* Www.wolterskluwer.com. https://www.wolterskluwer.com/en/expert-insights/risk-appetite-and-risk-tolerance-whats-the-difference

Maverick, J. B. (2021). *5 reasons why dividends matter to investors.* Investopedia. https://www.investopedia.com/articles/investing/091015/5-reasons-why-dividends-matter-investors.asp

Mohan, P. (2021, September 13). *6 key metrics every dividend investor must track.* Sharesight. https://www.sharesight.com/blog/6-key-metrics-every-dividend-investor-must-track/

Nagar, A. (2022, August 6). *Donald Kilbride's tips to achieve great success in investing - Keep it simple!* The Economic Times. https://economictimes.indiatimes.com/markets/stocks/news/donald-kilbrides-tips-to-achieve-great-success-in-investing/low-turnover/slideshow/93389359.cms

Nickolas, S. (2019). *Equity REIT vs. mortgage REIT: What's the difference?* Investopedia. https://www.investopedia.com/ask/answers/052815/what-difference-between-equity-reit-and-mortgage-reit.asp

O'Shea, A., & Lam-Balfour, T. (2022, November 21). *What Is a dividend?* NerdWallet. https://www.nerdwallet.com/article/investing/what-are-dividends

Price, M. (2022, July 1). *The dividend growth model: What is it and how do I use it?* The Motley Fool. https://www.fool.com/investing/stock-market/types-of-stocks/dividend-stocks/dividend-growth-model/#:~:text=What%20is%20the%20dividend%20growth

Reiff, N. (2022, November 9). *Qualified dividend.* Investopedia. https://www.investopedia.com/terms/q/qualifieddividend.asp

Royal, J. (2022, June 1). *10 best retirement plans in 2020.* Bankrate. https://www.bankrate.com/retirement/best-retirement-plans/

Segal, T. (2019). *Fundamental analysis definition.* Investopedia. https://www.investopedia.com/terms/f/fundamentalanalysis.asp

Shackleford, D. (2021, October). *What is risk appetite? Understanding the concept and how to use it.* SearchSecurity. https://www.techtarget.com/searchsecurity/definition/What-is-risk-appetite

Srivastav, A. K. (2019, March 20). *Dividend growth rate (meaning, formula) | How to calculate?* WallStreetMojo. https://www.wallstreetmojo.com/dividend-growth-rate/

Sukheja, B. (2022, November 20). *"Hold onto your money": Jeff Bezos warns of recession, advises people not to buy TV, fridge this holiday season.* NDTV.com. https://www.ndtv.com/world-news/hold-onto-your-money-jeff-bezos-warns-of-recession-advises-people-not-to-buy-tv-fridge-this-holiday-season-3536961

Sullivan, B. (2020, October 19). *Guide to dividend investing for beginners.* Forbes Advisor. https://www.forbes.com/advisor/investing/dividend-investing/

Vyas, R. (n.d.). *Step-by-step approach to retirement planning.* Www.personalfn.com. https://www.personalfn.com/guide/retirement-planning-steps#best-spproach-to-retirement-planning

*What is a dividend growth model? - Definition | Meaning | Example.* (2017). My Accounting Course. https://www.myaccountingcourse.com/accounting-dictionary/dividend-growth-model

*What is dividend growth investing & how does it work?* (2021, October 20). Www.titan.com. https://www.titan.com/articles/what-is-dividend-growth-investing#toc-5

# Image References

barbhuiya, T. (2021a). [HD photo by Towfiqu barbhuiya]. In *Unsplash.* https://unsplash.com/photos/jpqyfK7GB4w

barbhuiya, T. (2021b). [HD photo by Towfiqu barbhuiya]. In *Unsplash.* https://unsplash.com/photos/yIIFNiEKkYI

Dent, J. (2020). *White and blue glass-walled high rise building.* In *Unslpash.* https://unsplash.com/photos/w3eFhqXjkZE

Graham, S. (2016). [Person holding pencil near laptop computer]. In *Unsplash.* https://unsplash.com/photos/5fNmWej4tAA

Grey, A. (2018). [1 USA dollar banknotes]. In *Unsplash*. https://unsplash.com/photos/8lnbXtxFGZw

Harp, K. (2019). [Three assorted US dollar banknotes]. In *Unsplash*. https://unsplash.com/photos/QqAkoMIN5Jk

Howell, E. (2020). [Pink flower on white background]. In *Unsplash*. https://unsplash.com/photos/VlTJdP8ZY1c

Mallorca, T. (2019). [White and red wooden house miniature on brown table]. In *Unsplash*. https://unsplash.com/photos/rgJ1J8SDEAY

Mayo, J. (n.d.). [MacBook Pro on brown wooden table]. In *Unsplash*. https://unsplash.com/photos/HASoyURgPMY

micheile dot com. (2020). [Green plant in clear glass vase]. In *Unsplash*. https://unsplash.com/photos/ZVprbBmT8QA

Muza, C. (2016). [Laptop computer on glasstop table]. In *Unsplash*. https://unsplash.com/photos/hpjSkU2UYSU

Nygård, A. (2020). [Brown and white paper bag]. In *Unsplash*. https://unsplash.com/photos/OtqaCE_SEMI

Robbins, C. (2020). [Black remote control on yellow surface]. In *Unsplash*. https://unsplash.com/photos/ihqB-c8C7Bc

Sargu, V. (2017). [Two men playing chess]. In *Unsplash*. https://unsplash.com/photos/ItphH2lGzuI

Shaw, E. (2019). [Man and woman talking near the wall]. In *Unsplash*. https://unsplash.com/photos/VLkoOabAxqw

Sikkema, K. (2019). [Black android smartphone near ballpoint pen, tax withholding]. In *Unsplash*. https://unsplash.com/photos/M98NRBuzbpc

Spiske, M. (2021). [HD photo by Markus Spiske]. In *Unsplash*. https://unsplash.com/photos/SeicBzZXdRg

Stern, M. (2020). [Savings image]. In *Unsplash*. https://unsplash.com/photos/1zO4O3Z0UJA

Thought Catalog. (2017). [Person holding ballpoint pen writing on notebook]. In *Unsplash*. https://unsplash.com/photos/505eectW54k

Valery, J. (2019). [100 US dollar banknote]. In *Unsplash*. https://unsplash.com/photos/lVFoIi3SJq8

Made in United States
Orlando, FL
13 November 2023

38895617R00068